The road of human self-salvation

WU WEN

DEDICATION

In today's world, mankind is facing more and more serious and more frequent natural disasters, facing the bottomless struggle within the human race, facing the mutual cause and effect of natural and man-made disasters, intertwined with each other, especially major natural disasters such as climate change. And large-scale war, enough to destroy the entire human race.
Humanity has reached the threshold of life and death.
The main purpose of this book is to uphold the philosophical concept of revering nature and following the laws and trends of nature, and to explore the path of lasting peace and prosperity for mankind at all levels of thought, culture, economy, politics, and military affairs, with a view to attracting valuable insights and communicating with people. Together, we will explore a road to human redemption.

CONTENTS

ACKNOWLEDGMENTS

Thank you for God's blessing and my teacher's teaching. Because of my poor English level, the English version of this book will have many language problems. Thank the readers for their tolerance. I also expect professionals to translate this book from the Chinese version into the English version in the future.

FOREWORD: REFLECTIONS ON THE RUSSIAN-UKRAINIAN WAR

1. Justice

Justice has the following two meanings.

1. Respect nature, conform to nature, abide by and follow the laws and trends of nature, move towards inevitable success, and make oneself, others, society and all things harmonious and win-win.

2. Do things that are beneficial to the widest range of people and the well-being of the entire human society, and maintain the normal order of the entire human society.

People live in nature, and people are only an extremely small part of nature. The laws and trends of nature have an impact on people and human society everywhere. In the face of the laws and trends of nature, human and human society are those who obey it full of vigor and those who oppose it perish.

The development process of human civilization is also a process of human society moving towards democracy, freedom and equality, because only a more democratic, free and equal society can conform to the laws and trends of nature, and can accommodate more people and more people's needs of the wide range of activities.

Therefore, in modern society, dictatorial countries often have all industries withered and people's livelihood is difficult, and dictatorial countries often have full ideals and skinny reality.

Therefore, dictatorship is contrary to the laws and trends of nature and the way of heaven.

This is theory and it is fact!

Dictators often exploit, deceive, and brutally repress their own people, because all ideals are not for the well-being of the people, but for their own interests and ambitions.

A dictatorial country often does not follow the rules, because it is neither legal nor advantageous in the face of the rules, and it can only play hooligans. A dictatorial country destroys the normal order of the international community and damages the well-being of people in other countries.

The dictator is the cancer of the entire human society and the public enemy of all the people. The existence of the dictator is the shame of human civilization.

It's a theory, and it's a fact!

2. The army

Any country in the world with a strong military is a threat to other countries and will make other countries sleepless.

Every country in the world has a powerful army, which is a threat to all countries and will make all countries sleepless.

Under the leadership of the sense of opposition, the security of one's own country and organization is often built on the basis of the sleeplessness of other countries and organizations.

NATO has expanded to Russia's doorstep, Russia's dorm room is uneasy, and a nuclear power is still like this. Ukraine is at the border with a nuclear power. If it is not unsafe, why would you want to join NATO for asylum? Russia is sleepless, but as a nuclear power with the second largest military force in the world, who would easily start a war with it? How much of the invasion of Ukraine was really in the interest of the Russian people and the country? Didn't the anti-war demonstrations of the Russian people fully illustrate this?

As a product of the US-Soviet hegemony, should NATO withdraw from the stage of history after the disintegration of the Soviet Union? If NATO withdraws from the stage of history and faces a powerful Russia, will European countries also have trouble sleeping?

The army composed of people's sons, husbands, and fathers as the main force, and the army supported by people's hard work, has become the greatest threat to the entire human society!

This is a problem of the entire human society, and it should be solved at the level of the entire human society, not by a country brazenly launching a war.

In today's era, only the United Nations can justifiably represent the entire human race to resolve international disputes and safeguard human justice. Only by taking the United Nations as the main body and realizing the humanization of the military can we stop wars between countries and make all countries and all people feel at ease.

3. War

The essence of war is cannibalism within the human race, a crime committed by some people against another, and war is a tool of evil!

The initiator of the war, from the moment it raised the butcher's knife, it ran counter to justice, and only evil was left in its world!

When Russia invaded Ukraine, it was Putin, the dictator, who raised the butcher's knife against the Ukrainian people and the Russian people, because in this war, not only Ukrainians but also Russians died.

When Russian war criminals threaten the world with nuclear war, it means that they have lost their most basic humanity and become real devils!

The participants in the war all think they are righteous, and they all have reasons, but no matter how many reasons, they cannot cover up the essence of evil! In this world, only the United Nations and the people of the world have the right to represent justice.

Because of the veto power, the UN Security Council has lost its basic function of suppressing war and maintaining justice, making the UN useless!

In the process of ending World War II, the five permanent members made great sacrifices and made great contributions to the post-war world security, but this does not in any way hide the harm of the veto power to the authority of the United Nations and the normal order of human society. Looking at the history of the exercise of the one-vote veto power, it can be found that most of the time the one-vote veto power is protecting the private interests of the relevant countries, or even covering up evil.

Justice is like air and water. It seems cheap and easy to obtain, but it is indispensable to everyone. Without justice in society, everyone will fall into misery. Justice and evil are a pair of natural enemies, justice takes a step back, and evil takes a step forward. People are often insensitive to minor and partial (occurring in others) evils, and even gloat in misfortunes, but they don't know that their own behaviors will lead to the spread of evil, and ultimately they cannot be spared.

War is the product of the loss of justice to the extreme, and it is also the highest form of evil. In war, everyone is a victim. Even the dictator who initiated the war will eventually pay a heavy price for his actions.

Ukraine's resistance is to suppress violence with violence, and to repay evil with evil, but this is a helpless choice after the entire human society has lost its basic function of suppressing war and maintaining justice.

When the entire human society loses its basic function of restraining war and maintaining justice, and ending war resistance with war, it becomes justice.

The international community's sanctions against Russia are aimed at cutting off part of the supply and demand chain in human society, killing one thousand enemies and self-destructing eight hundred, and at the cost of economic depression and social unrest in the entire human society.

Although sanctions against Russia are a way to resolve the war, their evil is no less than that of a war, because its victims are more extensive and its impact is more far-reaching.

It is foreseeable that in the near future, at least most of the people will feel the hardship, and the people of Ukraine and Russia will be even more difficult.

The root of all this is the war madmen headed by Putin. It is their selfish interests and ambitions that have brought the entire human race into a situation of suffering and evil.

In the Russian-Ukrainian War, we saw that while the international community was trying its best to stop the war, it was also trying its best to avoid the destructive three world wars and nuclear wars.

For human society, the real enemy is not the Russian people, nor the pathetic Russian soldiers, but the Russian dictator.

The dictator is the cancer of the entire human society and the public enemy of all the people. The existence of dictators is a disgrace to human civilization.

Only by awakening the consciousness of the human race, expanding the power of the United Nations, abolishing the five permanent members and one veto power of the Security Council, and gradually realizing the humanization of the military, can the justice and normal order of human society be truly maintained, and the cancer of human society - dictators and war criminals will be eliminated.

Only by distinguishing Putins from Russian soldiers and Putins from the Russian people, and by uniting the Russian soldiers and Russian people, can we remove the cancers—dictators and war criminals—for human society at the least cost.

Only by classifying dictatorship as a crime against humanity, establishing a legal basis for eradicating dictatorship, and including overthrowing dictatorship as a category of nominal and material rewards, can we clear the entire human race against dictatorship.

4. Repent

There is such a story in the Bible, to the effect that: a woman was caught in adultery, and the crowd brought her to Jesus to demand punishment, and Jesus said, "He who is without sin among you, let him be the first to throw a stone at him. After the crowd left, they realized that no one had condemned her, and Jesus said, "I will not condemn you either, go! Do not sin again from now on."

War is the product of the irreconcilable development of contradictions, a dying struggle.

The Russian-Ukrainian war was firstly rooted in the loss of human society's basic function of suppressing war and maintaining justice, and secondly, it was rooted in the stubborn national consciousness of various countries. Under the leadership of national consciousness, each country was fighting with no bottom line and no justice standards.

All participating countries believe that they are just, but it is these so-called, selfish and narrow "justices" that have brought mankind into the abyss of war and turned a good human society into hell.

In today's globalization, when human beings face life and death due to environmental problems, human beings seem to have become adults with an IQ of only one or two years old, and can only allow each component of their body to go their own way and fight with each other, both insensitive and powerless.

If it is human misfortune to perish in natural disasters, then perishing in three world wars is human tragedy!

Everyone loves their country, nation, organization, but it is these countries, nations, organizations that impose war on people and turn the world into hell.

In this sense, in today's highly developed human civilization, patriotism, nationality, and organization are sins, and each of us is a sinner.

What power does a sinner have to convict another sinner? !

Therefore, God said: "I will not condemn you either, go! Do not sin again from now on", "The kingdom of heaven is near, you should repent!" ".

For the peace and normal order of human society, and for the well-being of all people, we should define "justice" from the height of all mankind, safeguard justice, and repent of our past mistakes.

The Bible says, "I tell you, this is more joy in heaven for one sinner who repents than for ninety-nine righteous who need not repent. "

Putins have committed greater sins than us ordinary people, but this does not mean that they have no right to repent. On the contrary, God prefers Putin's repentance.

For human society, Putin's repentance will allow human society to obtain the greatest benefit at the least cost. Their repentance is the most valuable!

Therefore, human society should use enough tolerance and pressure to accept and urge Putins to repent.

5. Heroes

In today's globalization of human social life, in today's frequent occurrence of natural disasters, and in today's extremely powerful weapons, a hero is a person who stands up or even sacrifices himself in the face of natural disasters ; a hero is a person who defends mankind. Peace and justice, the well-being of the people who come forward, even those who sacrifice themselves.

On the Russian-Ukrainian battlefield, because human society lost its basic function of suppressing war and maintaining justice, those soldiers who rose up to resist the Russian invasion of Ukraine played a role in resisting the war and maintaining justice. Ukrainian soldiers are heroes.

On the Russian-Ukrainian battlefield, those Russian troops who wielded slaughtering knives at the same kind, no matter how they are viewed in Russia, but in the eyes of other countries and all mankind, they are demons.

On the Russian-Ukrainian battlefield, Russian soldiers are the most pitiful and pathetic crowd. For the Putins, they are just tools and cannon fodder for slaughtering the Ukrainian people and realizing their own interests and ambitions. Their bloodshed and sacrifice cannot exchange for a trace of pity and true love from the Putins; for Russia, their bloodshed and sacrifice are exchanged for What came was the hatred, isolation, and sanctions against Russia by the international community. In exchange, all industries in Russia were withered and the people were struggling. For relatives, their sacrifices meant that parents lost their sons, wives lost their husbands, and children lost their fathers, their sacrifice, in exchange for the hardships of their loved ones.

No matter how much the state apparatus touts them, their bloodshed has no real meaning, and there is no trace of justice, they are just abandoned, pitiful demons.

It is right for soldiers to obey the orders of their superiors. Otherwise, the army will lose its order, soldiers with weapons will become a disaster for society, and the army and soldiers will lose the value and rationality of their existence.

But if the superior has become a dictator or an accomplice of the dictator, executing the order becomes a crime; refusing the order becomes justice; eliminating the dictator and his minions becomes a supreme honor!

It was Putin, the dictator, who turned the Russian soldiers on the Russian-Ukrainian battlefield into pitiful and pathetic demons.

For Russian soldiers, stopping the war of aggression is justice and justifying their own name; ending Putin's dictatorship is glory and revenge for themselves!

In fact, the army is the most fundamental support and tool of the dictator. Without the support of the army, the people of no country will accept the evil dictatorship. In this sense, it is the military who maintain the criminal dictatorship.

Soldiers have the responsibility and obligation to make amends for their own mistakes and end the dictatorship of their own country, which is also the mission and obligation of the military.

CHAPTER 1: INTRODUCTION

1. The theme of this book

In today's world, mankind is facing more and more serious and more frequent natural disasters, facing the bottomless struggle within the human race, facing the mutual cause and effect of natural and man-made disasters, intertwined with each other, especially major natural disasters such as climate change. And large-scale war, enough to destroy the entire human race.

Humanity has reached the threshold of life and death.

The main purpose of this book is to uphold the philosophical concept of revering nature and following the laws and trends of nature, and to explore the path of lasting peace and prosperity for mankind at all levels of thought, culture, economy, politics, and military affairs, with a view to attracting valuable insights and communicating with people. Together, we will explore a road to human redemption.

2. Philosophy

(1) The world of people and people

1. Naturally

The Bible says, "I am the true vine, and you are the branches; he that abides in me, and I abide in him, bear much fruit; for apart from me you can do nothing."

The real scene of people in nature is like a leaf falling in a lake. It seems to be free, but in fact everything is involuntarily. All human thoughts and behaviors seem to be independent, but in fact have their profound, precise and objective motivations .

Every act of man in the world (including thinking and doing) will cause more or less changes in the elements of the system related to this act. The accumulation of such changes over time will strengthen some aspects of people's thinking, behavior and even the structure of human life, while others will weaken or even eliminate them.

Different intensities and different times of accumulation have different degrees of accumulation in one existence. For existences with a high degree of accumulation, the lower the threshold for obtaining resources and channels, the easier it is to be called by the system. When the accumulation reaches a certain level, they will have a chain reaction with normal perception and behavioral activities. It will pop out automatically. For example: conditioned reflex.

Subjective consciousness is the result of this kind of accumulation. Because it is highly accumulated, it always appears in people's perception. Today, when science has been relatively highly developed, it is easy for people to find that through the interaction between existence, existence can be realized. To explain it by the change of motion, it just can't find its existence.

Subjective consciousness arises from this cumulative process and is the result of the interaction between the human nervous system and the outside world. Fundamentally speaking, there is no subjective consciousness, everything is natural, everything comes naturally.

2. Co-creation

Everything about human beings is a natural creation of nature, everything about human beings is involuntary, and human subjective consciousness is the result of the interaction between human nervous system and the outside world, and it is an illusory existence.

The so-called real awareness of people in this world is actually in the awareness of changes in themselves, especially the nervous system. There is no ultimate reality in everything in the human world.

The so-called existence of everything in the human world is the result of the "karmic origin" shared by humans and all things in this world. In other words, everything in the human world is the co-creation of humans and this world.

3. Cognitive way

The world based on the "karmic origin" of people's cognition style and existence style is closely related to people's cognition style and existence style.

Discrimination is the beginning of human cognition. It artificially distinguishes things that were originally one, so all things have shapes, properties, and even beauty, ugliness, good and evil, and the world has become a world where all things are interdependent and cause and effect. connected world.

People can only realize one thing at a time, and the things that people realize are always based on its shape, nature, even beauty, ugliness, good and evil, and the object of enlightenment is change, so everything in the human world is in a state of being, the state which In the process of movement, change, birth and death.

Human consciousness has a purpose, so the human world contains a way to realize it.

4. Idealism or materialism

The reason why people can distinguish objective things is the premise that objective things can be distinguished and can cause people to distinguish. That is to say, although the human world is closely related to the way of cognition and existence of human beings, the natural world can be recognized in this way, and the appearance and evolution based on this way of cognition and existence can be realized, is the premise that the way of cognition and the way of existence can be realized.

Therefore, the way of human cognition and the way of the world can appear according to this way of cognition, and the way of human existence and the way of the world can evolve according to this way of existence. In the world where human beings and all things in the world share create, there are not only subjective elements of human beings, but also objective elements of all things.

So, as far as epistemology is concerned, both idealism and materialism are imperfect .

Because man is a negligible existence compared to nature, and man is only a very weak member of the countless things in nature, so man does not occupy a dominant position in the world he participates in creating, On the contrary, in the world, people are like a small boat on the lake, and everything can't help themselves.

Therefore, for people, materialism is more reliable than idealism.

5. Road

For any one thing, from the perspective of it, its whole is a process of "birth, living, dissimilarity", and a process of interaction and mutual change between it and all things.

Maybe the world does not exist in a process way, but the world that people can perceive exists in a process way, so the human world exists in a process way. Perhaps this world does not need a purpose, but human consciousness has a purpose, so the human world must contain a way to achieve it.

For any one thing in the world, in the process of mutual karma between it and the world, what it faces is the whole world, and it is weaker than the whole world. Therefore, no one thing will occupy a dominant position in the process of the appearance and evolution of this world.

Therefore, Road , because it includes existence and its laws, also includes the way of realization, and realization itself is a process. As the "ultimate existence" of the human world, it is really suitable.

The Road is the natural path, the path that leads to the destination.

Therefore, in the human world, everything must follow the natural path and rules in order to achieve the goal and get a good ending.

Therefore, for everything in the human and human world, those who follow the path and rules of nature will prosper, and those who do not will perish.

(2) Truth

More than 2,000 years ago, there was a period of great ideological explosion on the earth. Christian thought, Buddhist thought, ancient Greek philosophical thought, and pre-Qin thought mainly represented by Taoism and Confucianism exploded. This period of thought exploded , which has laid a solid foundation for the development of human civilization.

Although, in modern society, science has led human civilization into a highly developed stage, but in terms of core concepts, science has not achieved breakthroughs. On the contrary, the current level of science has not yet reached the level of proof or overthrow those core concepts.

In this world, all human ideas are imperfect, and they have not yet reached the standard of truth. In this world, all the persistence of people are not completely right, because things will always be unexpected.

Therefore, the longer the path and the wider the scope of human thought and behavior, the more deviations from the truth and facts.

Of course, imperfection means that there is an element of truth in it; incompleteness means that there is an element of heaven in it.

Therefore, the continuous accumulation of human thoughts and actions is also a step by step approach to the truth and the way of heaven.

Therefore, the power of science does not lie in its strict logic, but in the constant revision of its theories through scientific experiments, so as to remove the false and retain the true, step by step closer to the truth and the way of heaven.

Therefore, science is the most effective and accurate cognitive means for human beings at present, although it still has a long way to go for human civilization.

(3) Need

Nature has nurtured all things, ranging from galaxies and celestial bodies, to all things on the earth, and to the microscopic world. Every place in nature is full of vitality and splendor.

Human cognition has a purpose. In order to achieve these purposes, people need to understand the movement and change of all things, the driving force of birth, living, and death.

A legitimate, self-consistent driving force is need.

All things are born out of the needs of nature, and all exist and grow because of the needs of nature. The movement and change of all things, the birth, living, dissimilarity and death are the results of this need to promote. Life is that nature needs you to live, and death is that nature needs you to die.

All things are born out of the needs of nature, they have acquired their own innate nature, and they have acquired the innate duties (missions) that nature has given them. their own innate nature produced their's thought and behavior.

For one of all things, the needs of nature are the combined force of the needs of all things in nature outside of itself. All things are created to meet this need, and obtain the basis for survival and growth.

As a result, this world has become a world in which all things in the world communicate with each other and satisfy each other, and become a world in which everything in the world is interdependent and causally related.

(4) Self-organization

In the process of intercommunication and mutual satisfaction of all things in the world, the world has a natural self-organization, and the common karma of everyone creates (creates) a wonderful world.

It is precisely because of this natural self-organization that things that exist naturally have extremely delicate perfection and adaptability to their environment. This is in stark contrast to the things that humans create under the guidance of their own obsessions.

Therefore, we can see that in the environment of freedom of thought and speech, great ideas and speeches that are useful to society are easy to appear; under the market economy system, people exchange their needs and satisfy each other through product exchanges, so that The entire social economy is prosperous, and everyone can benefit from it; in a democratic country, all social strata and groups communicate smoothly, and social conflicts can be resolved in a timely manner (will not let social conflicts rise to the level of large-scale brutal killings in autocratic countries.), all walks of life are thriving, and the whole society is full of vitality.

In contrast, autocratic countries are dead and silent, the economy of the entire society is becoming more and more depressed, people's lives are becoming less and less secure, social contradictions are constantly intensifying, setting off a wave of evil.

The root cause is that the former is dominated by the self-organization of nature, while the latter is dominated by people based on interests.

Therefore, respecting the self-organization of nature and making human society full of vitality is very important for the long-term existence and prosperity of human society.

3.The reshaping of values

All the excellent values of human beings have a common goal, the well-being of the people and the long-term existence and prosperity of human society.

Human beings also have many evil values. They start from satisfying the inflated selfish desires of certain minority groups, to kidnap and fool people, and exploiting the weaknesses of human nature as their means, with the goal of squeezing and enslaving the people, and committing crimes in human society, made A lot of sin.

In modern society, all kinds of values guide people's thoughts and behaviors in a specific group of people.

They have a common feature, that is, they all believe that they are correct and the supreme truth.

Therefore, under the guidance of these values, people take it for granted, with a sense of justice and sanctity, to compete with other groups of people under the guidance of values, and even struggle with no bottom line, and finally use violence and war to cause a war A tragedy, a crime committed.

These various values have made a fundamental mistake, that is, they believe that they are the supreme truth.

They all ignore the insignificance of human beings in front of nature, ignore the fact that human beings are just a small boat on the lake in nature, forget the fact that they can do nothing without nature; forget that in the human world, The fact that everything must follow the natural path and rules in order to achieve the goal and to get a good ending.

Therefore, truly mature values must have two basic characteristics: first, following the natural path and rules; second, aiming at the well-being of the people and the long-term existence and prosperity of human society.

In today's world, human beings are facing two major problems of more and more frequent and serious natural disasters and bottomless struggles, especially climate warming and war, which are major hidden dangers that can directly lead to the demise of human beings. Humanity has come to the crossroads of life and death.

Fundamentally speaking, the predicaments that human beings face are caused by problems with human values. The values of the free world lack enough reverence and observance to follow the natural path and rules, while the values of the authoritarian world lack all the two basic characteristics of mature values.

Therefore, the main purpose of this book in this regard is: for the values of the free world, in addition to analyzing the rationality of its origin from nature, it emphasizes the importance of natural paths and rules, so that people can change their values. so as to guide people to respect nature, follow the path and rules of nature, live in harmony with all things in nature, and realize the well-being of the people and the long-term existence and prosperity of human society ; In-depth analysis and severe criticism are made on the values of the authoritarian world, so as to awaken the people's awareness of its evil nature, awaken the dictator's conscience and abandon it.

4. Culture, economy, politics, military

This book holds a basic affirmative attitude towards the values of the free world, as well as the cultural, economic, and political systems of the free world.

This book advocates introducing the paths and rules of nature into the cultural, economic, and political aspects of the free world, so as to increase the maintenance of the natural ecological balance by human beings and the care of all things in nature, in order to resolve the continuous aggravation of natural disasters and realize human beings,living in harmony with all things in nature, realizing the well-being of the people and the long-term existence and prosperity of human society.

This book provides an original definition of justice, clarifies the natural connection between the ways and rules of nature and justice, knowledge, and science, and advocates introducing the ways and rules of nature into the cultural, economic, and political aspects of the free world to strengthen Social justice advocates the involvement of scientists in human politics and decision-making processes.

This book judges competition and struggle according to whether the natural road and rules are observed or not. It advocates that the vitality of human society can be improved through competition in the fields of thought, culture, economy and politics, but it is opposed to struggle. Combining competition with preserving the diversity of nature and human society, this book opposes any monopoly and dictatorship in ideology, culture, economy and politics.

The military aspect is very crucial. This book proposes the humanization of the military (including the humanization of nuclear weapons), in order to help solve the threat of war and the bottomless struggle within human beings. At the same time, this book also clarifies that a world dictatorship will give human beings It will bring irreversible and catastrophic consequences, so it is advocated to strictly prevent the emergence of a worldwide dictatorship in terms of values and human social organization mechanisms.

5. Love and Repentance

Is human nature good or evil? There has been an endless debate in the ideological circle, and there is no consensus.

Starting from the original sin of the Bible and analyzing the limitations of human cognition, this book draws the following conclusions:

The course of life is largely the accumulation of selfishness, stubbornness, greed, and sin.

In the human world, selfishness, stubbornness, greed, pain, and sin are always prominent, while mutual love, tolerance, peace, happiness, and kindness are always fleeting.

Humans and human society need to consciously and uninterruptedly abandon evil and promote good, so as to move towards a better future.

Note: Of course, the selfishness of the driving force of life is also a very important factor.

Based on this, this book proposes abandoning evil and promoting good from the conscious level of individuals and groups (it has a large similarity with self-cultivation).

Based on the above, this book proposes the "redemption of love" on the external level according to the Bible.

Regarding faults and sins, this book discusses the Christian thought of repentance, the Confucian thought of rectify, and the Buddhist thought of almsgiving, and focuses on the great significance of repentance, aiming to persuade people to correct their mistakes and tolerate the faults of others. , to give others the opportunity to reform and create a better future together.

Finally, this book persuades people to forget past hurts and sins, and not to harm others and themselves, through the discussion of the accumulation of sins from their own harm.

6. Awaken the consciousness of the human race

Awakening the consciousness of the human race is an important part of this book.

In today's world, mankind is facing more and more serious and more frequent natural disasters, facing the bottomless struggle within the human race, facing the mutual cause and effect of natural and man-made disasters, intertwined with each other, especially major natural disasters such as climate change. And large-scale war, enough to destroy the entire human race.

Humanity has reached the threshold of life and death.

This book discusses the natural conditions and basis for the awakening of human consciousness from three aspects: understanding one's most basic and natural characteristics, the fundamental difference between human beings and all things, and the significance of human society to a person.

This book discusses the relationship between human consciousness and the human world, discusses the emergence, illusory nature, important role, and limitations of subjective consciousness, and focuses on the evil of national consciousness, elicits the necessity of awakening human consciousness, and then discusses In order to awaken the consciousness of the human race, what should the human and human society do?

Based on the above, this book throws out the most important point - the expansion of the power of the United Nations.

CHAPTER 2: ALL THINGS IN THE WORLD ARE CONTAINED IN NATURE, AND ALL THINGS IN THE WORLD BELONG TO NATURE

1. Respect for nature

The progress of science has created a splendid human civilization, and it has also contributed to the arrogance of human beings.

Before science took hold, people believed that there were heavenly gods overhead and hell-hungry ghosts underfoot.

Therefore, people have the need to pursue goodness and beauty, and also have the fear of falling into misery.

Therefore, people have the power to constantly improve and repent!

Therefore, people at that time would not be too arrogant or too presumptuous!

Science has never denied theology, and modern science is far from reaching the point where it can challenge the core ideas of theology! Therefore, truly great scientists will not deny the existence of God, and many even believe in God.

Only all living beings who have tasted the sweetness of scientific development, all living beings who have little understanding of science, and all living beings who are kidnapped by greed, are desperately denying the existence of God!

Science has changed people's impression of the world, but it has not fundamentally changed people's world view.

Science has told people how small man is compared to the earth, how small the earth is compared to the Milky Way, and how small the Milky Way is compared to the universe. To his own insignificance, but instead gave birth to the dream of man conquering the sky!

Science has told people how people come from, how people's thoughts come into being, and what the relationship between people and everything looks like. However, poor sentient beings have given birth to stubborn self-consciousness, and think that they are born to enjoy boundless freedom and endless fun, and regard everything as resources, and frantically seize and plunder!

"In the beginning there was the Road, the Road was with God, and the Road was God.

"Jesus said, I am the way, the truth, and the life . No one comes to the Father except through me.

"I am the true vine, and you are the branches; he who abides in me, and I abide in him, bear much fruit; for apart from me you can do nothing."

--"Bible"

From the above-mentioned words in the Bible, we can understand that God is nature, the way and rules of nature, the truth of this world, existence itself, and life itself.

The real scene of people in nature is like a leaf falling in a lake. It seems to be free, but in fact everything is involuntarily. All human thoughts and behaviors seem to be independent, but in fact have their profound, precise and objective motivations.

All things in the world are contained in nature, and all things in the world belong to nature. Man is nothing without nature, and man can do nothing without nature.

The Bible says, "I am the true vine; my father is the gardener. He cuts off all the branches that are attached to me, and which do not bear fruit; and the branches that bear fruit, he prunes, so that it bears more the fruit"

How many attempts have mankind gone through since its birth to the present? How much repentance took place? How much suffering did we suffer? How much blood was lost? Only by adapting ourselves to this ecological environment can we make our civilization as splendid as it is today!

Could it be that today's people, for those useless obsessions, for those arrogant and selfish greed, still do not repent even though their heads are broken?

Do people today have to wait until they perish before leaving tears of remorse and helplessness?

Could it be that the meaning of human existence is to leave lessons for the next, higher species?

2. Morality

(1) Morality

"Road is a natural path, in which there are cause and effect, laws, and all things. Road generates all things, and it is the way people organize cognition . The survival and survival of the Road are the natural needs of the Road.

"Virtue, that is, obtaining the Road, is the reason and evidence for the existence and growth of all things. Virtue always follows the road. the Road generates all things, and it is based on needs. Virtue is that as an individual thing (person) obtains to make itself survive, The need for growth is to maintain and strengthen the needs of nature for oneself. The method is to fulfill the responsibilities and obligations that nature has given to oneself, and to do some good deeds that can be rewarded in the law of causality. Therefore, the meaning of virtue in traditional Chinese culture is basically It is equivalent to making contributions and doing good deeds. Virtue is not about obtaining things, nor is it plundering or occupying things and interests. If you can't get things right, you can't keep things, because that thing only belongs to the existence that produces and maintains it, need. "

The Road is the natural path, the path that leads to the destination.

Therefore, in the human world, everything must follow the natural path and rules in order to achieve the goal and get a good ending.

Therefore, for everything in the human and human world, those who follow the path and rules of nature will prosper, and those who do not will perish.

Like all things, people are created because of the needs of nature, and they are also able to grow and develop because they conform to the laws and trends of nature and make their due contributions to nature and all things in nature. Otherwise, they will lose their own value of existence and be destroyed and eliminated by nature.

The most important thing for people to live in this world is to fulfill the responsibilities entrusted to them by nature, to make their due contributions to nature and all things in nature, and to exchange this contribution for their own existence and development. Other than that, there is nothing good for me anymore.

Taking needs as the driving force and meeting the needs of others and other things as the behavior guide is the fundamental way of nature, the fundamental way of all things in the world, and the true meaning of morality.

(2) Social Rules

In human society, all religions have precepts, all countries have laws, and all human organizations and groups have rules.

Social rules, rooted in the natural road and rules, are combined with social interest structure and demand. The former comes from nature, from heaven and the latter from people.

Nature does not give special care to people and their society, so the paths and rules of nature may not be suitable for human survival. It is important to emphasize here that there is no achievement of goals without following the natural paths and rules.

The social rules that come from people are determined by the structure and needs of the society. Generally speaking, they have the function of maintaining the survival and development of people and society, but they may not conform to the paths and rules of nature, nor are they consistent with the survival and development of people and society.

Therefore, if human beings want to solve the current predicament and realize the long-term survival and development of the human race, the social rules of human beings must be adjusted with the progress of human cognition of natural roads and rules (mainly the progress of science) and the changes of human social structure and needs. The basis of adjustment is natural roads and rules, the motive force of adjustment is based on the needs of human social structure, and the bottom line of adjustment is that it cannot harm the survival and development of human beings.

In fact, human social activities are a natural adjustment of social rules. Even without the active adjustment of human society, the connotation of social rules is quietly changing. We have seen that with the development of human society, many new words will appear, many outdated words will be diluted, and the meanings of words will change with the development of the times, so that the social rules relying on words will change. form a new annotation. We have also seen that with the development of human society, the importance of some social rules will gradually emerge, while others will gradually fade or even be directly abandoned.

In an open, liberal and democratic society with moderate competition, the natural adjustment of social rules will become more and more conducive to the development of society. Because in such a society, the paths and rules of nature are always the paths and guidelines for all social activities, and the paths and rules for people and groups in society to achieve their own needs are the paths and rules of nature, so they can better adapt to Natural roads and rules, so as to achieve common development with the whole society and live in harmony with all things in nature.

On the contrary, in a closed and unified society, there is always a strong and stubborn force that is desperate to maintain its own greed, and is trying to cut off the natural path and rules and the connection with the people. Therefore, the longer such a society lasts, the more and more serious problems will arise , until serious class confrontation occurs, and brutal wars break out, thus causing social division.

Since such a split comes from war, the army occupies a very important position in the social group (small country) after the split. As a result, the social group (small country) after the split still cannot form a normal society, the ruler For the sake of their own interests, they squeezed and repressed internally and launched wars externally. As a result, troubled times appeared.

In troubled times, enlightened rulers will give the people more freedom and power, implement measures for recuperation, and use the natural paths and rules to play a role again, use the restoration of the way of heaven, and the society will prosper rapidly, so the rulers Under the support of strength, complete the reunification of the entire society (country).

what is this? This is the cyclical law of Chinese history. This periodic law not only has the same change process, but also has great similarity in the durations of the great unified dynasties and chaotic times. Of course, there is an exception. The Song Dynasty, because of its emphasis on literature and light on martial arts, has been in the confrontation of foreign tribes for a long time, but the result is that it perishes in the hands of foreign tribes.

At the same time, through the historical changes of ancient China, we can see that in the totalitarian society, the extreme selfishness and greed of the ruling class have caused extreme hatred of all social classes. By looking at the population numbers before and after the change of dynasties in Chinese history, we see the shocking and brutal killings caused by this hatred!

This shows that in a totalitarian society, the ruling class is selfish, greedy, and deviates from the natural path and rules, which has the characteristics of annihilating conscience and being irreversible to death!

Although the social rules of human beings may not all be correct or beneficial to human beings, as the historical precipitation of human social activities and the historical precipitation of human adaptation to nature, they must have a large amount of correctness and benefit.

Therefore, social rules can only be fine-tuned safely. Any radical and fundamental change will bring disaster to human society. Therefore, the revolution, just like its name, destroys human life, and the revolution will not build a beautiful society as people imagined, on the contrary, it will only become a catastrophe for the society.

Therefore, immature human groups and countries often carry out drastic social changes frequently, but they cannot achieve the long-term stability of society and the well-being and expectations of the people, bringing social disasters one after another, but they are always in the whirlpool of disasters. struggle.

Therefore, dictators often take the initiative to launch a social movement one by one, through the impact of the social movement on the normal social order, to block the accumulation of social justice, to destroy the growth of the enemy, and to shape the people into what he wants. slaves, thereby consolidating the dictatorship.

Finally, because social rules have a large number of correctness and advantages, and because there are no social rules to restrain, evil will not be restrained, it will spread, and it will cause chaos and disasters in the entire society. Therefore, people should abide by social rules, maintain social rules, for themselves, and for the sake of their peers.

(3) Dignity and shame of life

Human beings live in this world, perform their duties entrusted by nature, make their due contributions to nature and all things in nature, and exchange such contributions for their own existence and development is the dignity of a person's life.

Human society In nature, human beings belong to one kind of all things. Humans live in human society first. Therefore, exchanging one's own contribution to others and society in exchange for one's own existence and development is the main part of a person's dignity in life.

Therefore, don't try to get something for nothing, and don't settle for alms.

In the world, people cannot always conform to and conform to morality. There will always be faults and difficulties, there will always be times when they rely on the contributions of others and society, and there will always be times when they need explanations from others and society.

As the saying goes: "When you drink water, don't forget to dig the well, and the kindness of dripping water is reciprocated by the spring." People should remember this kind of contribution and help, and in the years to come, use their own contributions to others and society to repay this kindness. .

For a person, it is a shame to be born to rely on the contribution and help of others and the society for a long time with peace of mind.

In the face of social rules, people who are always in a state of being fed, just like those who are always in a state of exploitation and plunder, are all a shame for a human being.

Society should also have corresponding mechanisms to maintain social fairness and rules. A mature society is a society in which most people can live and work in peace and contentment, a society without a large number of people who are in a state of hunger and thirst, and a society without dominant people who are in a state of exploitation and plunder.

(4) Morality and freedom

Russo said: "Man is born free , but he is everywhere in chains. He who thinks he is the master of everything else is more of a slave than everything else . "

Today's people seem to only remember "people are born free", but not the following words. Therefore, people think that they are born to enjoy boundless freedom and endless fun, regard all things as resources, and frantically seize and plunder! And forgot to violate the shackles of nature-morality.

So, I remembered this passage:
People are fascinated by greed,
cannot love each other,
can not love all things,
unable to perform the duties assigned by nature,
so,
Disasters come one after another,
People suffer as groups!
People are short-sighted,
Can't see the truth of all things,
Can't see the cause and effect of things,
Can't see the relationship between man and nature,

so,

Blame the disaster on God,

Put the blame on fate.

People wailed in groups in the disaster, but after the wailing, they did not reflect or repent, and still went their own way.

People have never thought that their own food, clothing, housing and transportation, and their endless enjoyment, in fact, are the demands and destruction of all natural things and natural ecosystems. People haven't measured whether their demands and damages to all natural things and natural ecosystems are equal to their guards and contributions to all natural things and natural ecosystems.

People have never thought that when everything in nature has been destroyed in large quantities, when the natural ecosystem has suffered unprecedented damage, and when the entire human race is facing the crisis of extinction, it is already a sin to live, let alone extravagance and wanton enjoyment? People have not compared, what is the difference between human beings now, compared with nature, and cancer cells, compared with a patient?

People have not thought that when human beings are extinct, will the sun still rise from the east of the earth? Will there be a living world on Earth again? The answer is yes, the extinction of human beings is only the extinction of human beings and the things that depend on them, not the destruction of the entire world. People have not compared themselves with the dinosaurs before extinction, what is the difference?

Therefore, we cannot talk about freedom without morality. Please note: Morality here refers to the laws and trends of nature, as well as human contributions to the natural ecosystem and all things in nature.

Of course, the value of liberty is great, and the greatness of liberty will be discussed in subsequent chapters.

3. Justice

(1) Justice, knowledge, and science

The so-called justice is to do things that conform to the laws and trends of nature, and are blessed by gods, and will inevitably succeed. Where there is justice, there will be evil. The so-called evil is to do things that do not conform to the laws and trends of nature, and are not blessed by gods , something that is bound to fail.

When a person does something, whether it is righteous or evil depends not on who shouts louder or who has more power, but who does what is in line with the laws and trends of nature and is blessed by the gods and successful thing.

A person's goal-oriented behavior is rooted in and based on people's cognition. Without a correct cognition of things, their motions, and changing laws, people cannot control their own behaviors and the results of their behaviors.

Therefore, whether a person can do justice depends on whether he can obtain and rationally use the knowledge of things and their laws of motion and change, that is, whether he can achieve knowledge.

So, knowledge is the root of justice. Since knowledge is the root of justice, whoever has knowledge represents justice.

The justice of social behavior lies in whether or not to master the knowledge of the laws of social development and change. Modern society is a society with a high degree of division of labor. It is impossible for everyone to spend his life time and energy studying the laws of social development and change. Just like it is impossible for everyone to spend his life time and energy producing cars, social division of labor not only enables people to have different jobs, but also enables people to acquire different professional knowledge. A farmer can hardly build a house better than a construction worker. A construction worker can hardly give lectures better than a teacher. It is difficult for a teacher to cook better than a chef ... Therefore, it is difficult for us ordinary people to know this society and its changing rules better than intellectuals.

"Knowledge" is the precipitation of "things and their laws of movement and change" in life. Knowledge deposited in life has paved a path in life that conforms to its laws, and has gathered Potential energy who develop and change along this path. Therefore, when a person thinks about one thing and does one thing, he will consciously or unconsciously move forward along this road. When a kind of knowledge is precipitated in life, the more profound it is, the more The more accessible the road, the stronger the potential energy it gathers, and it will affect people's judgments and choices，The road it has paved is the person's character. When a kind of knowledge accumulates more and more in life It will gradually become the master of this life. At this time, people will not consciously defend this knowledge, so that "the rich and the noble cannot be promiscuous, the poor and the lowly cannot be moved, the mighty cannot be subdued", or even "kill the body to become a benevolent", and sacrifice for it precious lives.

In this world, nothing is closer to the laws and trends of nature than science, and no one is closer to justice than scientists.

Respect for nature, respect for morality and justice, make contributions to natural ecosystem and all natural things, help mankind to be on the verge of extinction, and enable mankind to survive and develop continuously, which can not be separated from science and scientists.

Human beings have gone from primitive society to today's highly developed civilized society step by step, which has made a qualitative leap in the spiritual and material living standards of each member, and even civilization has become the fundamental symbol that distinguishes human beings from other species.

Fundamentally speaking, all kinds of progress of human society are rooted in knowledge and the cognition of the laws and trends of nature. It is with the understanding of the laws and trends of nature that human beings can grow step by step and expand their living space step by step on the premise of complying with the laws and trends of nature, so as to develop into today's highly developed human civilization.

Respect for prophets is a powerful driving force for the development of ancient human civilization; respect for science is a powerful driving force for the development of modern human civilization.

In the history of human beings, any anti-intellectual behavior has brought a lot of evil, deep suffering, and social regression.

For people and human society, justice is like air and water. Under normal circumstances, it is very cheap and almost negligible, but if it is missing, it is fatal.

Justice is to do things that conform to the laws and trends of nature, and are blessed by gods, and must succeed, and vice versa is evil, and there must be one or the other between justice and evil. Therefore , the lack of justice must be accompanied by the advent of evil.

Humans act out of their own needs, and Humans become conscious because they realize their own changes, which contains the limitations of human nature and human consciousness. Just as people will not work hard for air and water, just as a board hits someone else's butt without feeling pain, only when misfortune happens to oneself can one deeply appreciate the importance of justice.

Therefore, it is the basic responsibility of human beings and human society to consciously maintain justice.

(2) Always do what is appropriate and right

People's thoughts and behaviors are driven by their own needs, but not all needs and the actions of the people it drives can arouse conscious awareness.

Therefore, many human actions are unconscious and purposeless.

The interaction between humans and all things in nature is happening all the time, and the human perception system can only perceive a small part of it.

Therefore, in the social practice of human beings, there are many actions of oneself, and there are many influences of the outside world on oneself, which cannot be perceived or realized.

The present of man is the result of the accumulation of past life activities. Life is a process, and in this process, many things are often "missing by the slightest, and by a thousand miles".

Therefore, people should always do appropriate and correct things to accumulate more normal and precise interactions with all things in nature, so that their life structure can be more coordinated with nature and all things in nature, and let themselves the path interact with all things in nature action is smoother. In this way, his actions are unwittingly justified.

On the other hand, if a person always goes his own way regardless of external conditions, always goes the wrong way and does things not according to common sense, and always sneaks up tricks and tricks, it will lead to the incongruity between one's life structure and nature and all things, which will lead to one's the way of interaction with all things in nature is blocked. In this way, He is sure to do something wrong by doing it, there is no justice at all.

From another perspective, maintaining the roads and rules of nature, maintaining the normal order of human society, enabling people to do appropriate and correct things, and fulfilling the responsibility that human society should bear for the justice of the actions of its members, It is also where the justice of human society lies.

(3) Historical truth and freedom of speech

The so-called justice is to do things that conform to the laws and trends of nature, are blessed by the gods and are bound to succeed. When there is justice, there is evil. The so-called evil means doing things that are not in line with the laws and trends of nature, are not blessed by the gods, and are bound to fail.

History is the evolutionary process of nature. In the human world, nothing is more in line with the laws and trends of nature, more blessed by the gods, and contains more justice than the truth of history.

Therefore, another source of justice lies in people's cognition of historical truth.

The present of man is the result of the accumulation of past life activities. Therefore, the cognition of the truth about the things related to oneself in the past is very important to whether people can do "things that conform to the laws and trends of nature, are blessed by the gods, and are bound to succeed", that is, the understanding of people's actions Justice is crucial.

The original intention of a dictator is to kidnap, oppress, and enslave the vast number of people; the essence of a dictatorship is to rape the way of heaven and humanity, to destroy the normal social order of mankind, and to be an evil existence.

Therefore, the first thing that dictators do is to cover up the historical truth, and the most fearful thing is the historical truth, because the historical truth can lead to justice.

Nature is self-consistent, and historical truth is self-consistent. It can be recognized in many ways. On the contrary, lies are not self-consistent, and they can be broken through many ways .

Therefore, dictators must restrict people's freedom of speech, because the truth is always difficult to hide, and this society will never lack the wise.

Since "the present of man is the result of the accumulation of past life activities", so, in the past life activities, people have accumulated a lot of justice unconsciously, so people naturally know right and wrong, good and evil.

Therefore, human life activities are the accumulation process of justice, and the majority of people naturally have genes against dictatorship.

A normal society must respect the truth of history, safeguard people's freedom of speech, allow natural paths and rules to pass in human society, and let justice fill the world.

Knowledge is the representative of justice, but only in the environment of freedom of thought and speech, because only in this environment can knowledge constantly correct itself and bring itself closer to the truth and true justice. On the contrary， only to ossify step by step, deviate from the natural path and rules, and run counter to truth and justice.

4. Peace the world

Man's survival depends the balance on the environment and various factors in his own life, And the balance is within the limits that man can bear, and on the long-term stability . Balance is the premise that the form of things can be stable. Without this balance， It will continue to change, not to mention normal life activities, let alone the realization of goals. For example, a person wants to do some work, but the temperature fluctuates constantly between -5 degrees and 30 degrees. Although this temperature change is within the limits that people can bear, people must take timely measures (such as putting on and taking off clothes) according to the temperature change. At this time, people cannot work with peace of mind.

"Balance" can have two meanings. First, the environment and various factors in one's own life are balanced within the limits that people can bear, so that people can live safely. Second, in order to realize "all kinds of factors in the environment and one's own life are balanced within the limits that one can bear", one has to take concrete actions (for example, to balance the world).

Therefore, the object of ' Balance the World ' in "The Great Learning" is not just human society, but all things in the world.

With the progress of human society, the influence of human beings on the environment has also been greatly increased, which has brought unprecedented changes in the living environment, and factors that can threaten the existence of human beings have also appeared, such as ecological environmental protection issues, nuclear weapons issues, and climate warming， AI problems, etc.

Based on the needs of human existence and development, the interaction with all things in heaven and earth can make each other interact harmoniously and win-win, and reduce or even eliminate the behaviors that harm others and themselves. This is accompanied by the progress of human society, which is the responsibility and obligation that human beings must bear.

The biggest feature of cancer is that the reproduction of cancer cells is not restricted by the human immune system. Selfish cancer cells multiply wildly in the human body, and frantically plunder and destroy other parts of the human body and the human ecosystem. As a result, all cancer cells and the human body perish together.

The relationship between cancer cells and the human body is very similar to the current relationship between human beings and nature.

People's survival depends the balance on the environment and various factors in their own life, The balance is within the limits that people can bear, and on the long-term stability.

For people, society, all things, and nature, any factor that is not restricted by the ecosystem is a cancer.

For people, all kinds of stubborn obsessions, desires, and pursuits that can make people desperate are cancer.

For society, Monopoly in any field is a cancer. Ideological autocracy, economic monopoly, political dictatorship, military hegemony, etc, are all cancers.

For nature, human beings who do not know how to care for all things and maintain the natural ecological balance, and things that destroy the natural ecological balance are also cancers.

Therefore, if a person wants to be happy and long-lived, and a society wants to have long-term stability, he must get rid of all cancers in himself and the external environment, and contribute to the ecological balance of himself and the external environment.

5. Equality

"Heaven and earth are not benevolent, and all things are dogs. Saints are not benevolent, and people are dogs. "

- "Tao Te Ching"

Nature has its own way of existence and laws of operation, and it is not dependent on human will, nor does it have special care for someone or something, a certain type of people or something.

From the perspective of the overall operation of nature, nothing is superfluous. The birth, living, and death of all things, and the birth, aging, illness and death of people are all the needs of nature.

All things and people are an integral part of nature, the products of nature's needs, all have their own innate attributes due to the innate mission that nature has given them, and they are all born out of fulfilling the innate mission that nature has entrusted to them. to survive.

There is no fundamental difference between all things and all people in nature, and there is no distinction between high and low.

Therefore, people should not have prejudice or discriminatory thoughts and behaviors against anyone or anything.

Therefore, everyone and everything should have the freedom and opportunity to exert their natural attributes.

What needs to be emphasized here is that equality does not mean complete equality, equality is equality under the paths and rules of nature.

One cannot make an adult and a three-year-old eat the same amount of food for equality.

People can't in order to pursue equality, divide bread and water equally between a hungry person and a hungry person under the condition that there is only one bread and one water, so that both of them can't be satisfied ...

The greatest evil of human beings is to abandon the laws and rules of nature and pursue the so-called absolute equality and fairness.

They can't see the natural path and rules, the paths and rules of social wealth generation, they only focus on the existing social wealth, take advantage of people's pursuit of equality, engaging in the so-called killing the rich and helping the poor, or absolute equal distribution, Even engaging in the so-called communism. This is the biggest mistake in the development of human society.

"Power cannot be privately owned, and property cannot be shared, otherwise mankind will enter the door of disaster. "

—— John Locke, "On Government"

"The way of the people is also. Those who have permanent property have perseverance, and those who do not have constant property have no perseverance. If they do not have perseverance, they Will become evil and extravagant， and selfish "　　　　　　—— "Mencius Teng Wen Gong Shang"

Property is the reward for fulfilling the mission entrusted by nature, the goal of man's actions to meet his own needs, and the material condition on which man lives.

Humans have fulfilled the mission entrusted by nature, made contributions to meet the needs of nature (including all things in nature and others), and received corresponding rewards. This is the way and rules of nature.

Without the natural path and rules, without the path and rules of social wealth generation, the output of social wealth will be severely shrunk, and people will slowly have nothing to eat. Therefore, under the above model, people are very happy to eat meat on the first day, eat rice noodles without meat on the second day, but they are still in a good mood because of fairness, and on the third day, they can only eat wild vegetables and grass roots， depressed, the wild vegetables and grass roots disappeared on the fourth day, and all the evils in human nature were stimulated, so the hell on earth appeared.

Humans make contributions to the satisfaction of the needs of nature (including all things in nature and others), and receive corresponding rewards to meet their own needs. This is the path and nature of human beings.

Property is a material condition for people to live on. If people cannot reasonably own it, people will inevitably break through all the rules to obtain it. This is the compulsion of the survival situation.

Without the path and nature of human beings, the natural relationship between contribution and acquisition, power and obligation will be severed, society and people will lose their reasonable path and order, and the human nature of being lazy will be released. If the need is not met, then all evil will be released.

If the above conditions persist long enough, it is enough to change the nature of man, and not the nature of individual people, but the nature of nearly all people. Therefore, when I see unruly and immoral old people, I often hear such a sentence: "It's not the old people who get bad, it's the bad people who get old".

Therefore, "absolute equality, absolute fairness, and public ownership of property" violates the natural path and rules, and violates the human path and rules, forcing people to break through all rules and use all dirty and sinful means to obtain It is necessary to make the whole world full of evil.

"Don't suffer from few but suffer from unevenness" is the result of horizontal comparison between people, and it is the immature disposition of people in the absence of natural, human paths and rules. When it is used by careerists and conspirators, there will be a large number of followers, thus forming a terrible trend of thought.

"Absolute equality, absolute fairness, public property" is so grandiose that people have no reason to question or refute it, so that it has become ideologically correct and politically correct, so that people still maintain its authority despite suffering and doing evil things.

"Absolute equality, absolute fairness, and public ownership of property" is so evil that it will not care about the life and death of the majority, so that it will produce an interest group composed of a very small number of people who firmly maintain its existence to As for it will kidnap the entire society into the extremely bloody and brutal Songun regime.

As the saying goes, violence is always a desperate struggle when there is no way to go, and it is always the final form of all evil.

6. Liberal democracy

We put our hope in great monarch and cast our rights into a sword and hand it over to him, so that he can uphold justice and exorcise evil, but unexpectedly, under the the order of nature and the environment of life, he only represents himself, and the sword has also become a way to drive us away to a tool of suffering.

The national prosperity, the people suffer, the national crisis, the people die, we have struggled between suffering and death for thousands of years, and we have no regrets so far.

In this world, the creation of all things is rooted in the needs of nature, and all things have a foothold in order to fulfill the mission entrusted by nature.

The creation of all things by nature is rooted in the need of nature to exert its own innate mission to all things and to contribute to nature and all things in nature, and this mission and need are actually the natural attributes of all things. Therefore, there is a saying in "The Doctrine of the Mean" that "the destiny is called nature".

The process of movement and change of all things and the way to realize the mission of innate talent are subject to the laws and trends of nature, their own natural attributes and external environmental conditions.

Therefore, all things in this world have their own unique paths to realize their innate mission.

The saying goes: Heaven has the way of heaven, earth has the way of earth, God has the way of the gods, ghosts have the way of ghosts, human beings have the way of things, and things have the way of things. There are 360 industries of people, every industry has its own way. There are different sizes of cars, and each type of vehicle has its own lane.

There is a saying in China: " Only the feet know whether the shoes fit or not." And this foot can only be his own foot, not someone else's foot. Shoes tried on other people's feet are always more or less incompatible with my own.

One's own innate mission is fulfilled by oneself; one's own innate attributes are exerted by oneself; one's own ideal pursuit is fulfilled by oneself. This is the normal way of life for all things.

Man is created by the needs of nature, and man takes his own needs as the source of all actions.

In this world, the active actions of all people are rooted in their own needs, and all others are independent of their own needs.

Therefore, no one should represent others, a group, a country, or even the entire human race. All people represent only himself.

Therefore, it is extremely stupid to place hope on others, hand over your own power to others, and let others realize the satisfaction of your needs and the happiness of life.

Therefore, it is an extremely vicious behavior to seize the power of others and not let go, to confuse black and white, to point the deer as a horse, to coerce and entice others to do whatever it takes, just to satisfy one's own desires, and wantonly oppress and enslave others.

Therefore, in a mature society, people must be free, because only with freedom can people unleash their innate attributes, correctly perform their innate missions, and make contributions to nature and all things in nature. People get what they need for life with their contribution. This is the way of heaven, and it is also the way of humanity.

Therefore, a mature society must be a democratic society, because only in democracy, social life will not be kidnapped by dictators, human social life will not violate the way of heaven and humanity, and human social life will have a normal order. And the various needs of all kinds of people in the society, has the normal way to meet the needs. Without democracy, society is left with fantasy, deception, kidnapping, and evil.

So, liberal democracy is the cornerstone of a mature, normal society.

Only on the basis of freedom and democracy can human politics and decision-making process correctly resolve real matters. Without freedom and democracy, morality and justice will be lost, and human society will become the feast cancerous. It is bound to have a tragic ending.

Therefore, everyone in this world should defend freedom and democracy, because freedom and democracy is the right way in the world, because dictatorship is a cancer in the world, because defending freedom and democracy is one's own duty and merit, because not defending freedom and democracy is one's own evil, disaster.

7. Competition

(1) The need for competition

People take their own needs as the source of all behaviors. When needs are satisfied, people will no longer have any motivation to act.

In a society with a very fine division of labor, people's driving force to work and contribute is what they need in their lives. When a person has a very comfortable life, he will no longer have the motivation to work and contribute.

Therefore, from a natural point of view, people are lazy and want to get more benefits and pay less hard work.

Therefore, in a society with fair rationing, output will always be less and less, people's living standards will always be lower and lower, and it will inevitably develop into a serious shortage of materials. When most people cannot meet the basic needs of survival, a large number of evils will breed. As a result, through all kinds of evils, the size of the population is reduced, and allocate what is left to people whose quantity is greatly reduced.. If things go on like this, the society will become more and more poor and weak.

In a society, when everyone eats corn and sweet potatoes, no one needs to eat meat. This is not because meat is not delicious, or because they do not know that meat is delicious, but because there is no hope of eating meat, only everyone is eating like this, so everybody accept own fate.

Therefore, in the pursuit of a so-called absolutely fair society, people often consciously or unintentionally transfer man-made disasters to nature.

Absolute fairness makes people lose sight of hope and difference, and makes people use despair and numbness to digest their own needs, creating an illusion of an ideal society, however, it is bound to bring the truth to the surface because people's basic needs are not met, and will lead to a great deal of evil.

Modern society is a society with a highly developed social division of labor. Whether a person is an official, a businessman, a scholar, a farmer, a worker, or a soldier... all have their own division of labor, their own posts, and their own responsibilities.

We have made our share in our position, in exchange for enjoying the fruits of others' labor. Maybe we just moved a few bricks on the construction site today, but it doesn't affect our ability to enjoy three meals a day, we can wear clothes to avoid being naked, and we can play mobile phones after work ...

In a society with a highly developed social division of labor, it depends on specialization and the mutual coordination and promotion of various professions, and on the prominence of people's various needs brought about by social differences, resulting in the improvement of people's labor enthusiasm, which is extremely The earth has promoted the improvement of the productivity of the whole society and the common prosperity of all walks of life.

Relying on the prosperity of the whole society, each of us can satisfy various needs through a single job, and the material living standard of an ordinary person is higher than that of the ancient emperors.

In a society with a highly developed social division of labor, we rely on our own contribution to live, and live on the labor results of our own in exchange for others labor results. We and other social members are essentially a symbiotic relationship.

Therefore, society needs appropriate differences, people need to see their own needs clearly from differences, and people need to work and make contributions for their own needs, so as to achieve a better life.

Therefore, society needs differences, and it needs to use the power of example to guide people to see their own needs and compete with each other in a reasonable way, so as to achieve a better future for themselves, others and even the whole society.

(2) The justice of competition

Everything in this world has its own unique path to achieve its natural mission and its own needs. The saying goes: Heaven has the way of heaven, earth has the way of earth, God has the way of the gods, ghosts have the way of ghosts, human beings have the way of things, and things have the way of things. There are 360 industries of people, every industry has its own way. There are different sizes of cars, and each type of vehicle has its own lane.

In human society, different industries, different jobs, and different lives have their own paths to achieve their natural mission and needs. And this road, given to us by nature, is the natural road and the most reasonable road.

Therefore, the justice of human competition is reflected in whether the competition is carried out under the rules of this road, and whether the competition is conducive to the common prosperity of related industries and even the whole society.

A bottomless struggle that deviates from this natural path and rules is extremely harmful to the prosperity of society and to the vast majority of people in society.

For example, people are divided by race, country, group, faith and class, and struggles with the goal of seizing, plundering and killing are often unable to realize their own ideals, but bring deep disasters to the whole society and most people in the society.

It is a very immoral behavior to lose sight of the symbiotic relationship among oneself, others and society, and to gain benefits by setting checkpoints and bottlenecks on others' way to realize their natural mission and their own needs. It is a trampling on natural roads and rules to make use of their own unique resources, force and other people's weaknesses to engage in coercive transactions.

When there are many people and many groups in this society, using the above-mentioned ways that deviate from the natural path and rules to fight each other, this society becomes a jungle society, and there is no civilization, let alone the future. .

(3) Limitation of competition

The scope of competition should be limited to natural paths and rules, and should not be mixed with man-made obsessions and greed. This is because only competition, which is now set within the paths and rules of nature, can lead to success and bring about the greatest social benefit.

This point has already been discussed in the previous section and will not be repeated here.

Limiting the scope of competition is actually limiting the competition to a just interval.

Like all things, human beings are created by the needs of nature, and they all grow and develop because they conform to the laws and trends of nature and make their due contributions to nature and all things in nature. Otherwise, it will lose the value of its own existence and be destroyed and eliminated by nature.

The driving force of the struggle is its own needs, and its path is to satisfy its own needs through plundering and harm. It violates the original intention of nature to create all things, violates the way and rules that all things in nature exchange their own contributions for their own needs, and tramples on the order that all things communicate with each other and interdependence. Is a departure from heaven and humanity.

Because the struggle violates the path and rules of nature and tramples on the normal order of all things, especially human beings, it has resulted in the decline of nature's capacity for both sides of the struggle, and the shrinking of their respective existence values, thereby strengthening and increasing their respective values and demand, which in turn increases the brutality of the struggle with catastrophic consequences.

Therefore, the nature of the struggle is evil, and the outcome of the struggle is disastrous.

Competition is not a struggle. Competition is in line with the natural path and rules, in line with the interests of society and participants, and its essence is justice.

Therefore, the limit of competition, the most fundamental and most important, is not to alienate and escalate to struggle.

Therefore, a normal society encourages competition and restricts struggle; while a dictatorial society encourages struggle, and as long as there is contention, it will be a life-and-death struggle.

Below we discuss the limits of competition from the following three aspects.

First, do not attack personally and do not upgrade to killing.

The most legitimate way for two people to compete for a position and a contract is for everyone to change and strengthen themselves to make themselves more suitable for the requirements of this position and this contract, and the selectors and society should ensure the process of competition, Confined to path and rules from nature of this position and this contract.

Only in this way can competitors be guaranteed to compete on the right path and in the right way; only in this way can the results of competition be guaranteed to meet the needs of this position and this contract to the greatest extent; only in this way can we maximize the social benefits,and in order to maximize the benefits of all parties involved (among them, the loser of the competition will get the maximum return of life experience, thus laying the foundation for future success.)

The misguided way of competition lies in personal attacks against competitors, through intrigues, and through other factors, to exclude competitors or even eliminate them, so as to win the competition.

In fact, in today's world, this kind of competition is quite common.

In democracies, both sides of an electoral contest tend to dig into the other's scandals, which are often unrelated to what the two sides are campaigning for, but which often have a big impact on the outcome of the contest.

This is because people often demand politicians with the moral standards of saints, but politicians are just ordinary people, and as long as they are human, they have human nature and have advantages and disadvantages. For a politician, the most important thing is his governance plan, political ability, and political responsibility, rather than the shortcomings revealed by the scandal, because those shortcomings have little impact on his governing effect .

Also because people like to capture these scandals to satisfy their bad temperament.

The ultimate root cause lies in the lack of people's sense of responsibility and attention to elections, a matter of great significance to society and themselves. In the matter of elections, there is a lack of compliance with the corresponding natural paths and rules. In other words, , is the lack of justice.

When most people are like this, a lot of problems arise.

Therefore, we have seen that many elections in a democratic society are full of chaos, and the results of the elections may not necessarily conform to the interests of society and the general public.

In an autocratic society, due to the lack of natural roads and rules, and the constraints and guidance of normal social rules and order, the justice and limits of competition cannot be guaranteed at all.

There are countless cases of "personal attacks against competitors, through intrigues and other factors to exclude competitors or even eliminate them, so as to win the competition".

For example, among the people who have no officials do not greed, eliminate dissidents through anti-corruption; When there is really no reason, people can be accused of whored ...

If a competition process allows the existence of this competition method, then for the relevant parties in the competition process, it is to bring wolves into the house and destroy the building; if a society allows the existence of this competition method, then this competition method will If it spreads like a cancer cell, the reasonable rules and order of this society will be destroyed, and eventually lead to catastrophic consequences.

Second, don't Intensify contradictions, don't kidnap the whole

Intensify contradictions, kidnap the whole, is to artificially elevate a limited competition to a major goal or rule of life, even to artificially elevate it to a more important and extensive standard and rule.

former is for example: a person, in the competition for a job, an opportunity or a love, cares too much about the result and ignores his other needs, other aspects. He will do everything in his power to win this competition, and if he loses in the competition, he will even end his own life.

In this example, the competition's place in a person's life has risen to the point of inexorability, and the person has been kidnapped by a competing whole in his life. His competition process will naturally go astray , which will inevitably lead to bad, even disastrous consequences.

The latter is the more terrifying Intensify contradictions and kidnap the whole. It comes from other competitors, outsiders, and even the public opinion to Intensify contradictions and kidnap the whole.

For example, one person said that the cherry blossoms in Japan are beautiful, but as a result, some or even many people said that he was beautifying the invaders, covering up the history of aggression, and betraying his ancestral country.

If a society is to let people arrested for speech one by one, with the help of small contradictions, it will set off a series of movements and struggles, which will not only destroy the reasonable rules and order of this society, and the people who will also be full of passion time and time again, is the people who will face a tragic outcome.

The most terrifying way to intensify contradictions and kidnap the whole, is to turn competition into violence, murder, and war, thus turning it into evil and disaster.

Good people and bad people have no words on their faces, and whoever raises the butcher's knife is the wicked person.

Whoever uses the weapon is the executioner; whoever uses it is the wicked person. As the saying goes, there is no good or evil, and the Road is divided into good and evil.

In the process of competition, whoever raises the butcher's knife first, who goes to the evil way first, and whoever escalates the competition into violence, murder, and war first, is the wicked one.

A mature society should have a mechanism for severely punishing such wicked people in order to maintain the justice and limits of competition and prevent the spread of evil.

Third, as things end, so should the competition.

A normal competitive relationship must end with the end of the competitive event. The competition that has lost its rationality and limits and has risen to evil "competition" will continue to maintain opposition and struggle after the competition event is over.

For example, two colleagues compete for a position. When the dust settles on the position, the superior party uses new resources to suppress and bully the other party, while the loser of the competition also harbors resentment and confronts and retaliates against the former.

The confrontation and struggle after the end of the competition is a departure from the natural path and rules, and it is a destruction of the normal rules and order of the society. A mature society should have mechanisms for prevention, identification, and disposal in this regard.

8. Diversity

(1) Natural diversity

In this world, there are innumerable galaxies, innumerable celestial bodies, innumerable species, and innumerable microscopic beings. Even humans are of all kinds, and no two are exactly the same.

In this world, all existence is rooted in the needs of nature. No existence is superfluous, and those that cannot meet the needs of nature will be alienated and perished in the next stage.

No matter how advanced science and technology are, people can only recognize things that are causally related to their own world. Even if there is one thing around people or even in people's bodies, as long as it can't lead to changes that can make people conscious, Humans cannot know; no matter how far away or different a thing is from a person, as long as it is causally related (whether directly or indirectly) to a change that produces enlightenment, it can be recognized.

Therefore, the world that people can recognize must be a world in which everything is causality-related, but causality-related is not necessarily natural reality. Because such a world is based on people's distinction between things, situation and attributes of things, and this foundation itself is artificial or may be wrong.

Discrimination of things, as the awakening of human consciousness and the origin of human beings, is reflected in many ancient human cultures. In fact, all human consciousness, cognition, and actions are based on the discrimination of things.

One separates and gives birth to the second, which describes the origin of objective things. The reason why people can distinguish objective things is that the objective things can be distinguished and can cause people to distinguish.

The objective things in the human world are objective things that exist in people's concepts and are the product of people's cognition. It is premised on the awakening of people's consciousness "that they can distinguish things". In this sense, people's discrimination behavior is a manifestation of the existence of objective things in the human world, or the existence of objective things in the human world, which is naturally based on people's way of life.

Although the causality of everything is not necessarily the natural truth, the world that can be cognized based on the way of human cognition and the way of existence of human life can only be a world in which everything is causality.

Therefore, everything in the human world is more or less, or directly or indirectly related to people. Everything in the human world, or more or less, or directly or indirectly, supports the existence of human beings; Everything in the human world is symbiotic and interdependent with others.

Therefore, to maintain the diversity of this world is to protect human beings; to care for all things that can be touched is to care for human beings.

(2) The diversity of human society

As the saying goes, "One flower, one world, one leaf, one bodhi", all things and people are facing the whole world related to their own cause and effect, and all things and people have the brand of the whole world on themselves.

All things in the human world are in motion and change, and they are all going through the process of birth, dwelling, dissimilarity and annihilation. Therefore, people must constantly change themselves and adapt to this world in order to survive for a long time.

In the human world, there are all kinds of people, groups, organizations, and countries. They all have their own unique way of existence. In particular, each country has its own unique cultural, economic, and political model. They all have meaning and value in their existence.

The history of mankind is a history in which different parts of mankind fuse, cooperate, compete and learn from each other.

Any ideological, cultural, economic, or political model of human society will become rigid, and will gradually decline or even perish if it does not accept mutual integration, cooperation, competition, and mutual learning with the outside world. Therefore, all the countries who cut off one's country from the outside world in human history have gone into decline, while all the countries who open and inclusive have all gone strong.

It is the different ways of survival of different parts of human society, which give other parts inspiration and opportunities to change themselves and adapt to nature.

Therefore, every individual, every human group, and even the entire human race must adhere to the values of tolerance and freedom, so that they are always full of vitality, able to change themselves in time and adapt to nature, so as to obtain lasting existence and development.

Of course, this does not mean that people and groups who are obviously anti-nature and anti-human are to be tolerated, because their very existence endangers the above ideas.

9. Reform and opening up is the great awakening of the Chinese nation

(1) Lost for two thousand years

In the process of the development of Chinese civilization, "removing a hundred schools of thought and respecting Confucianism alone" is a major historical retrograde event.

Because of the limitations of human cognition, any thought can't completely conform to the road and rules of nature and can't reach the standard of truth. Therefore, any thought needs to revise itself bit by bit during the collision with other thoughts and in practical practice, so as to keep its vitality all the time.

Confucianism is a very great thought. But without the collision of other ideas, Confucianism lacks the opportunity for self-correction, and can only lose its own rationality step by step in autism, leading the Chinese civilization it dominates to decline step by step.

Therefore, in the Chinese civilization after "removing a hundred schools of thought and respecting Confucianism", there were no thinkers and academic books of the pre-Qin level, and the thinkers and academic books of later generations were also inferior to each other.

Of course, the gradual decline of Chinese civilization is not only because of "removing a hundred schools of thought and respecting Confucianism alone", What's more, the so-called Confucianism in later generations is the result of the feudal rulers' selective use of Confucianism for their own personal gain and changing it into an anti-intellectual tool for fools, which is almost essentially different from the Confucianism in the pre-Qin period.

In the process of the decline of Chinese civilization, the two barbaric rule of Yuan and Qing era destroyed the last bit of rationality and backbone of Confucianism, and implanted the seeds of anti-intellect and servility in the genes of Confucianism and even the Chinese nation.

The declining Chinese nation has endured hardship and humiliation in modern times, but it has also recovered a little bit of vitality from the collision and fusion of Chinese and Western ideas. The Republic of China opened up people's wisdom and revitalized education, which made the Chinese nation once again have a large number of world-class masters. The Republic of China fought against foreign humiliation with a weak body, and finally won the five permanent seats in the United Nations and won the respect of the world.

However, the sad thing is that the toxins left over from history is so stubborn that, when combined with communist ideology, it has forcibly pulled China back into the vortex of misery and sin.

After enjoying a feast brought about by collective robbery, the Chinese people immediately entered an era of withering away all industries and starvation. Flowers and applause can make people emotional, but they can't satisfy everyone's hunger. In the era of broken rituals and music, the evil in human nature has been released unprecedentedly. The struggle of the whole people with no bottom line pervades the entire era. Fighting against others today, being fought by others tomorrow, fighting and being fought, shows the retribution of cause and effect. The art of emperors, which has been circulated for more than two thousand years, has been brought into full play in this era. The ignorant and ignorant people used their own suffering and bright red blood to cast a bright red crown.

Communism is a road that doesn't work at all, it's a fantasy that hides evil.

(2) Reform and opening up

1. Reform

Reform is not a revolution, but a gradual social change.

Looking at the population numbers before and after the change of dynasties in Chinese history, we see shocking brutal killings. Such cruel killing each other is extremely rare in the whole world history. China's traditional culture and the Chinese people's character and habits have determined that a revolution in Chinese society will mean more serious catastrophe and loss of life. Today, with advanced technology and advanced weapons, the consequences of a revolution in China are even more unimaginable.

Therefore, avoiding revolution in China is a major issue for the whole of China and even the whole world, and it is the well-being of all Chinese people and even all people in the world.

Therefore, the most important reason why the reform and opening up is great is that it is a gradual social change, which avoids a catastrophe and avoids ruins massive life.

Practice is the only criterion for testing truth, focusing on economic construction and not arguing, freeing Chinese society from the shackles of utopianism and moving towards social progress and people's well-being. In just 40 years, China's society has undergone earth-shaking changes, and the living standards of the Chinese people have been improved unprecedentedly.

Reform, there is only direction, no end; life, only better, not the best!

Those who wish to have a revolution in China should ask themselves, what are you doing? What kind of society do you want? What kind of life do you want?

Those who want China to go back to that era should put themselves in their shoes and think, are you willing to eat grass roots and bark? Are you willing to become a stupid and ignorant villain? Are you willing to be beaten to death?

Those who plan to lead China back to that era should ask themselves, where is your conscience? What is your own humanity? What is the difference between yourself and a devil? You should kneel in front of the statue of Yanhuang and repent to the ancestors, the dead and the living compatriots! Even more, you should try your best to correct your mistakes and use your own achievements to make up for your mistakes, so as to win the forgive of ancestors, so as to win the forgive of the hundreds of millions of compatriots, so as to win the forgive of the history , so as to win the forgive of the heaven!

2. opening up

Any ideological, cultural, economic, or political model of human society will become rigid, and will gradually decline or even perish if it does not accept mutual integration, cooperation, competition, and mutual learning with the outside world. Therefore, all the countries who cut off one's country from the outside world in human history have gone into decline, while all the countries who open and inclusive have all gone strong.

It is the different ways of survival of different parts of human society, which give other parts inspiration and opportunities to change themselves and adapt to nature.

The reason why China's reform and opening up has made great achievements is that in addition to putting aside disputes, putting aside the shackles of communism, and allowing society to return to justice and normality, it has integrated with the outside world, cooperated with each other, competed with each other, and learned from each other, to achieve win-win cooperation with countries around the world, is an important reason.

Chinese society has a distinct unity, and this unity has penetrated into all fields of thought, culture, economy and politics. This uniformity severely limits the dynamism of all areas of Chinese society.

The Confucian thought of "pruning and improving their own self-cultivation, unified family, good governance in the region, and finally make the world balance" has its applicable objects. The object of "pruning and improving" is the body, the object of unify is the family, the object of governance is the region (ancient vassal state), and the object of balance is the world (in the concept of the ancients at the time, this so-called world is far inferior to the current China Big).

In ancient times, feudal lords had various social strata and all walks of life. Therefore, "unify" could no longer be used for management, because "unify" would limit the performance of their respective responsibilities by people from all walks of life，would limit the vitality of the industry. However, the size of the vassal state is still relatively small, and a certain concept can be used to manage and guide it, so that people from all walks of life can play their respective responsibilities and people from all walks of life can live and work in peace and contentment.

In ancient times, although "the world" was small, it had a larger volume and a more complex structure. At this time, the concept of "no matter how good, beautiful and complete" could not make it possible to achieve social stability and could not make it possible to achieve all levels of society are full of vitality, which means that the method of "governance" is no longer applicable. At this time, it needs to be " balance" to deal with. " balance" means to eliminate the monopolist in any field and maintain the ecological balance of the entire system.

Therefore, the various dynasties in Chinese history, as long as they did not pursue the policy of "quiet and inactive, recuperate and recuperate", no matter what methods were used to manage them, they would inevitably decline.

In today's era, human civilization is highly developed, and the social structure is unprecedentedly complex. Even for a city, the method of "governance" is no longer sufficient. The idea of great unification is still more used in "unify and governance" to manage the country, and "unify" is greater than "governance". This is a serious mismatch of methods and objects.

Therefore, for Chinese society, opening to the outside world (that is, accepting and integrating with the outside world, cooperating with each other, competing with each other, and learning from each other) is the fundamental way to ensure social vitality.

CHAPTER 3: LOVE AND REPENTANCE

1. All things are born when they gain the Road, and they perish when they lose the Road .

In this world, the creation of all things is rooted in the needs of nature, and all things have a foothold in order to fulfill the mission entrusted by nature.

Therefore, everything that exists in nature is useful to nature and conforms to nature's path and rules.

However, everything in nature is going through the process of birth, dwelling, and death, and everyone in nature is also going through the process of birth, aging, sickness and death.

"Heaven and earth are not benevolent, and all things are dogs." At every moment of nature, only things that are useful and conform to the path and rules of nature have evolved and remain, while those that are useless and do not conform to the great The natural way and the rules of things are alienated and eliminated.

Therefore, the birth and dwelling of all things is the need of nature, and the annihilation is also the need of nature, that is, it needs its annihilation, or it does not need its existence. The same is true of human birth, old age, sickness and death.

Therefore, when all things attain the Road, they are born, and when they lose the Road, they perish. (Road means: in line with the laws and trends of nature, or in line with the roads and rules of nature, useful to nature, and able to meet the needs of nature)

Therefore, in order to survive and grow for a long time, the human and human society needs to constantly change itself, constantly adapt to the roads and rules of nature, constantly maintain the ecological environment on which it depends, and constantly serve the nature ,   contribution to the development and change of nature

Therefore, we can say this: man is innocent, because he still exists; man is sinful, and because he does not repent, he will be pruned and destroyed.

2. Original Sin

(1) The origin of consciousness

"But the serpent is more cunning than all the living creatures of the field that the LORD God has made. The serpent said to the woman, Did God really say that you must not eat of all the fruit of the trees in the garden ?

"The woman said to the snake, We may eat the fruit of the trees in the garden,

"Only the fruit of the tree in the garden, which God has said, you shall not eat or touch, lest you die.

"The snake said to the woman, you will not necessarily die,

"For God knows that in the day you eat, your eyes will be opened, and you will be like gods, knowing good and evil.

"Then the woman saw that the fruit of that tree was good for food, pleasing to the eye, and desirable, and wise, and she took the fruit and ate it. She gave it to her husband, and he also ate it.

"Then the eyes of both of them were opened, and they realized that they were naked, so they took fig leaves and made skirts for themselves.

"There was a cool breeze, and the LORD God was walking in the garden. The man and his wife heard the voice of God, and they hid among the trees in the garden from the presence of the LORD God.

"The LORD God called the man and said to him, Where are you.

"He said, I heard your voice in the garden, and I was afraid. Because I was naked, I hid.

"Who told you to be naked, says the LORD, did you eat the fruit of the tree that I commanded you not to eat?

"The man said, The woman you gave me to live with me, she gave me the fruit of the tree, and I ate.

"The LORD God said to the woman, What are you doing? The woman said, The serpent tempted me, and I ate it.

"The LORD God said to the serpent, Cursed thou, having done this, more than all beasts and beasts; and thou shalt walk on the stomach and eat dirt all the days of the day.

"I will make you and the woman enmity against each other. Your seed and the woman's seed will be against each other. The woman's seed will bruise your head, and you will bruise his heel.

"And I said to the woman, I will greatly increase your pain in childbirth, and you will suffer in childbirth. You will desire your husband, and your husband will rule over you.

"And said to Adam, Since you have obeyed your wife and have eaten of the fruit of the tree, which I commanded you not to eat, the ground will be cursed for your sake. You will toil all the days of your life so that you may eat from the ground. "

--"Bible"

The original sin of man lies in eating the fruit of discerning good and evil, and man becomes wise.

Discrimination of things, as the awakening of human consciousness and even the origin of human beings, is reflected in many ancient human cultures. In fact, all human consciousness, cognition, and actions are based on the discrimination of things.

In a world where there is no difference between everything and everything, things has no movement ,no change ,no produce, no maintain, no mutate, no destroy, and people has no birth, no old, no sick， no death, no good ， no evil, no happiness, no disaster.

When people can't distinguish the difference between all things, they won't have any thoughts and thoughts, it's impossible to recognize the world, and it's impossible to take any active actions.

Distinguishing the difference between things is the origin of human consciousness and the origin of human "autonomous" life.

(2) Original sin is hidden in people's cognitive limitations

It is human nature to appreciate and pay attention to the changing and moving unwholesome and unbeautiful things, and often ignore the things that have entered a normal, balanced and harmonious state.

People can only recognize things by distinguishing the difference between them.

Therefore, human cognition and life are full of differences and opposites of things, and the process of human cognition and life is constantly strengthening the cognition of such differences and opposites.

Therefore, the course of life is largely the accumulation of selfishness, stubbornness, greed, and sin.

Therefore, in people's cognition and life, the concept of difference and opposition between things is deeply rooted, and those beautiful and perfect things, because the difference is blurred, it is easy to withdraw from people's perception, cognition and even people' s life.

Therefore, in the human world, selfishness, stubbornness, greed, pain, and sin are always prominent, while mutual love, tolerance, peace, happiness, goodness and beauty are always fleeting.

So in the human world, good things don't go out, and bad things travel thousands of miles.

Therefore, in the human world, happiness is always fleeting, while the torment of pain cannot stop for a long time.

...

The fruit of distinguishing between good and evil allows people to gain wisdom and an "autonomous" life, and also allows people to walk into the abyss of sin and suffering.

Note: The so-called autonomy is just an illusion of a person after his consciousness is awakened. For the principle, please refer to "The Generation of Subjective Consciousness and Its Illusory" in Chapter 4.

3. Gratitude

(1) Born as a human being

"The LORD God made man out of the dust of the ground, and breathed into his nostrils the breath of life, and he became a living being, whose name was Adam.

"...

"The LORD God put the man in the Garden of Eden to repair it and keep it.

"The LORD God said to him, You may eat whatever you want from every tree in the garden.

"But you shall not eat of the tree of the knowledge of good and evil, for in the day you eat it you will surely die. "

--"Bible"

From the perspective of the Bible, man's position is the manager of the Garden of Eden, that is, the manager of man's world. People manage their own world and enjoy the various gifts of this world.

"Only heaven and earth are the parents of all things; only man is the spirit of all things. "

- "Book of Shang, Book of Zhou, Book of Thailand"

"Ling, the original meaning of the word creation: verb, when there is a severe drought, the shaman prays and prays for rain in a eloquent manner. "

- "Hieroglyph Dictionary"

Therefore, in traditional Chinese culture, human beings are the communicators of the origin and gods of the universe and nature.

"Book of Changes" talks about the three talents of heaven, earth and human beings. Its six lines, the bottom two lines are like earth, the two lines in the middle are like people, and the top line is like heaven.

Therefore, the top of man's head is the sky, and his feet are the earth. Man is an existence that stands above the sky and stands side by side with the heaven and the earth.

Compared with all things, people have more spirituality, more fun in life, and also have a larger mission and a larger life space.

Therefore, it is a very fortunate thing to be born as a human being.

Therefore, everyone should be proud and fortunate to be a person.

(2) Why are we people?

1. Genetics

The reason why a person is a person is that, first of all, he has inherited people's genes, and has people's material structure and temperament characteristics.

What kind of material structure there is, what kind of karma depends on.

What kind of material structure there is, what kind of karma depends on, what kind of way of life, what kind of disposition, what kind of thinking and behavior pattern.

A person, as a person, is based on genetic inheritance, based on his parents, his parents' parents, and even his ancestors from generation to generation.

Therefore, in Chinese traditional culture, "filial piety" is the foundation and the most important thing.

Therefore, "the Book of Filial Piety" says:

"Honour filial piety is the foundation of virtue, and the source of teaching is born.

Filial piety is the scripture of heaven, the righteousness of the earth, and the conduct of the people. "

2. Human civilization

In today's highly developed human civilization, any individual's contribution to this society is far less than what he gets from society.

In a position, if you do a little thing, you can get the solution of food, clothing, housing, and transportation, and even many people can get more and more expensive life enjoyment through this, which can benefit those who are close to them. Even people who have not contributed much can obtain basic necessities of life through social assistance.

The root of this "asymmetry" is that the development of human civilization has allowed people to catch the express train of natural evolution. In the process of conforming to the laws and trends of nature, human beings have obtained a large number of natural resources for life's required supply.

This "asymmetry" also stems from the refinement of social division of labor. The refinement of the social division of labor enables people to better understand and conform to the laws and trends of nature, and a large number of supplies from nature provides the necessary conditions ,which established a normal social order for exchange of existence, mutual satisfaction, and harmonious coexistence for people.

Therefore, people can obtain a large amount of life-needed satisfaction through a single, light-loaded labor.

On the contrary, for a solitary animal, the most basic satiety is difficult to satisfy, and it must spend most of its energy and time on seeking food in order to survive.

The fundamental reason for the rich material life that human beings can enjoy is not their own quality, let alone natural deserving, but the development of human civilization, and a society which people communicate with each other, satisfy each other, and coexist harmoniously.

Language and culture are the products of the development of human society, the co-creation of people's ancestors and the same kind, and also depend on the common support of all members of society to exist.

With the support of language and culture, people will have needs and enjoyments that are separated from the material level. More advanced, the life experience from the spiritual level makes people and animals have a significant difference in the quality of life.

Combining the first section, we can think that the reason why a person becomes a person is because he inherits his genes and lives in human society, which is also the fundamental difference between humans and animals.

3. The gift of nature

The right temperature, the right atmospheric pressure, sunlight, air, water, all kinds of food... Nature provides all kinds of balanced conditions and substances that human beings need for life.

Living in nature, human beings are almost in a state of "stretching out their hands with get dressed and opening their mouths with eat rice".

There are too many balanced conditions and substances that support the existence of human life, and people can naturally meet the needs of life without the need for people to acquire them deliberately.

There are also too many balance conditions and substances that need to be actively obtained by people. The materials come from nature, and the production process is not dominated by human beings, but is rooted in the natural evolution process of nature.

Agriculture is more prominent in this regard. People often only carry out some management behaviors such as ploughing, sowing, weeding, pruning, harvesting, etc., but "the real process of maturation from seeds to a large amount of food" is a natural evolutionary process.

Even for industry, its basic raw materials still come from nature, and its production process still has to follow the laws and trends of nature.

In fact, human beings have never existed and cannot exist independently of nature. The realization of all human goals and the process of satisfying all needs must take the existing conditions of nature as the starting point, and take the natural evolution of nature as the road (In fact, human beings achieve the goals and needs of life by "riding the express train of natural evolution").

Even people think that artificial manufacturing , also must follow the laws and trends of nature, and must rely on the natural evolution of nature to achieve.

Human beings are in nature, everything is just as the Bible says: "I am the true vine, and you are the branches; he who abides in me, and I abide in him, bear much fruit; You can't do anything without me. "

Everything about human beings, fundamentally speaking, originate from the gifts of nature.

(3) Human weakness

People can only recognize things by distinguishing the difference between them.

Demand is the driving force of all human life activities.

Therefore, human vision, thinking, and behavior are always chasing their own needs, and they are always struggling in the process of imperfection and unhappiness.

Because, when a need is met, people lose their ability to perceive it and their natural drive to maintain it.

A need that has been met, only when its balance is broken again will human beings feel its importance, regret, and cherish, but it is often too late.

Just like love, when it is not obtained, both parties will love unforgettable and desperate, and will make all necessary changes and sacrifices for the other party. Once obtained, everything will gradually return to plain, the originally hidden weaknesses and needs of the two sides will gradually emerge and become prominent. As a result, they forgot the pledge of eternal love, the seas run dry and the rocks crumble, and parted ways.

However, the satisfaction of a need, just because it has reached a state of completeness and balance, does not mean that it has disappeared. Therefore, the love that parted ways, because the original needs of life will appear again, thus leaving huge life shortfalls for both parties. Smart people will take action to restore, or actively change to find and cherish the next love; unsmart people will be heartbroken, broken jars, and go to a dark and tragic life.

In fact, most of the disasters facing human beings now originate from their crazy demands from nature, breaking some of the original equilibrium conditions suitable for human survival.

Human beings are accustomed to being gifted by nature, forget their own mission, and forget their responsibilities to nature and themselves.

(4) Gratitude

The beauty of life, the difficulty of being a human being, and the weakness of human nature are all calling for a grateful heart.

The gift already exists, and it must be digested in life, out of perception, out of need-driven.

A grateful heart is to review the past needs, to review the gifts of others, and to review the beauty of the process of satisfying needs.

A grateful heart is to create the need and driving force to maintain this beauty in this review and review, so that it can make concrete actions to maintain this beauty.

A grateful heart is helpful for people to keep the happiness and the beauty,what they have gained , and not fall into the grief of loss.

A grateful heart is conducive to people living in a peaceful, happy and beautiful state, and is conducive to improving the quality of life.

A grateful heart is conducive to dissolving the unwholesome and beautiful desires, needs, and impulses in life, so that people can get rid of the process of constant struggle in one sea of suffering, so as to reach the other side of the ideal.

4, abandon evil and promote good

Due to the limitations of cognition, with the development of human civilization, selfishness, stubbornness, greed, pain, and sin gradually accumulate in human and human society, while mutual love, tolerance, peace, happiness, goodness and beauty are gradually reduced. .

Therefore, people and human society need to consciously and uninterruptedly abandon evil and promote good, so as to move towards a better future.

(1) Don't to do evil because smallness, and don't not to do good because smallness

"Everything in the world is born of existence, and existence is born of non-existence.

"A tree that is hugged is born at the end of a millimeter; a platform of nine layers begins with a pile of earth; a journey of a thousand miles begins with a single step."

- "Tao Te Ching"

In the human world, everything is the result of the common karma of people and this world , as long as "karma" If the conditions are sufficient, one can create something out of nothing.

In this world, all existence originates from the needs of nature. As long as it meets the needs of nature, it can survive and grow. (As an aside: man is only a negligible part of nature, and what nature needs is not necessarily what man needs. Therefore, people hate Satan very much, but God didn't get rid of Satan because God needed it. Its evil can guide people to see God's goodness and spur people to be good constantly.)

In the human world, everything in the present is the accumulation of the past, and everything in the future is the accumulation of the past and the present.

Every action in life is like planting a seed. As long as the conditions are ripe, it will sprout and grow, and it will become a towering tree.

Therefore, a small indulgence will result in a huge mistake due to fate, and a small good deed will bring a big surprise due to fate.

The so-called karma is the accumulation and gathering of karma that can coexist in the same direction, thereby creating something out of nothing and suddenly achieving it.

(2) If there is no buying and selling, there will be no killing

Everything that exists in this world arises from need.

This need may be one's own, or it may be external, and the external need can be changed into one's own need through exchange. For example, when a person needs work, what he actually needs is to exchange the results of his work for his other needs, and the results of his work are external needs.

This is a natural and social process of mutual exchange and mutual satisfaction. It is the way of heaven and the way of humanity.

All evils in this society have their origins and reasons.

Therefore, all sins should not only be attributed to the person who raised the butcher's knife, but should also include those who prompted him to raise the butcher's knife.

Therefore, people should resolve, eliminate, and restrain their own bad needs, lest others raise the butcher's knife and involve themselves in sin.

(3) Open source and reduce expenditure

The process of people distinguishing things is accompanied by the collection of condition and attributes. When people distinguish themselves from external objects, they will find that there is a causal relationship between themselves and external objects, which is exactly how they feel about external objects, leading to changes that can lead to enlightenment, and this change is the result of the causal relationship between oneself and external objects. Things that have no causal relationship with themselves cannot lead to changes that can lead to enlightenment, so they cannot be realized or recognized.

Therefore, the world that people can recognize must be a world in which all things are causally related to each other, but the causal relationship between all things is not necessarily a natural reality.

Pangu's opening up of heaven and earth is separation, and the awakening of human consciousness is discrimination, all of which are accompanied by human actions. This action will inevitably result in the mutual relationship of "interdependence, interaction, interaction and relative movement and change equivalence" between separated things,this relationship is rooted in people's separation and discrimination of the originally integrated things, and also is a reply to the separation and discrimination actions. What we see is an indisputable fact: in the known world, everything is or directly or indirectly, or strongly or weakly interrelated, which can be recognized by people because of its equivalence and is restricting the movement and change of everything.

The world between people is an interrelated world, and all things in this world are all things that are interdependent and interact with people.

Due to the limitations of human cognition, things that are not causally related to themselves cannot lead to changes that make people conscious, so they cannot be conscious or cognition. Therefore, the human world is far from the whole of nature.

Even in the world of man, man is a tiny and negligible existence relative to him.

Therefore, the demise of mankind is not the demise of all things in the human world, nor the demise of the entire nature. On the contrary, human beings perish, not to mention nature, even the earth will still have various existences, a thriving scene.

Man's survival depends on the environment and various factors in his own life, the balance is within the limits that man can bear, and it also depends on the long-term stability of this balance.

All kinds of disasters that mankind is currently facing are rooted in the breaking of this balance, and ultimately rooted in the madness of Human claim for nature, and ultimately rooted in the destruction and destruction of all things.

Therefore, human beings should maintain this balance and cherish all things that also maintain them, because this is actually maintaining the existence and development of human beings themselves.

To achieve the above goals, there are two measures to increase revenue and reduce expenditure.

First: increase revenue

From the birth of human beings to the present, it is a process of gradual growth step by step, and this process is accompanied by a more in-depth and extensive intervention of human beings in nature, and a more direct and stronger interaction and interdependent between human beings and more and more things.

The fundamental reason for the current predicament of human beings is not the development and growth of human beings. In fact, with the development of human civilization, human beings are increasingly finding themselves insignificant relative to nature. Nature has enough stage for people to go to showing the chapters of life.

The fundamental reason for the current predicament of mankind is that mankind has lost the reverence for the paths and rules of nature. Driven by selfishness and desires, they have done too many evil things to nature, destroying and destroying all things in nature, resulting in the imbalance of their own demands and contributions to nature, resulting in changes in the ecological environment and the internal structure and order of the human race that are not conducive to the survival of the human race, resulting in an imbalance between nature's accommodating capacity for the human race and the existing scale of the human race.

Therefore, the fundamental way out for human beings to get out of the predicament and achieve better development is to make greater contributions to the ecological balance of nature, optimize the internal structure and order of the human race, and expand the capacity of nature to accommodate the human race.

All human efforts should follow the path and rules of nature, which also includes maintaining the values and social rules derived from nature.

To follow the natural roads and rules, the first thing is to know the natural roads and rules more correctly, which requires human beings to respect science and support the rapid development of science, especially the rapid development of disciplines that are beneficial to dealing with disasters, maintaining ecological balance and optimizing the internal structure and order of human race.

Second: reduce expenditure

Throttling is to reduce the demand of human beings from nature and the destruction and destruction of all things. It is also the most direct and effective means for human beings to reform themselves and deal with disasters.

All human actions are rooted in needs, and no matter how long the chain of supply and demand is, oneself is in this chain after all, and one's "greed" will go straight to the terminal along the chain of supply and demand. Therefore, without our own uncontrolled needs, there will be no other people's demands from nature, and there will be no other people's destruction and destruction of all things.

Therefore, everyone is responsible for the demands of nature and the destruction and destruction of all things.

Therefore, everyone has an obligation to curb greed, practice thrift, cherish all things, reduce human demands from nature, and reduce human destroy and destroy all things.

5.The redemption of love

(1) What is love

"Love is patient; love is kind; love is not envious or boastful or arrogant or rude. It does not insist on its own way; it is not irritable or resentful, it does not rejoice in wrongdoing, but rejoices in the truth. It bears all things, believes all things, hopes all things, endures all things. Love never ends."

--"Bible"

Because of the influence of original sin, in the human world, selfishness, stubbornness, greed, suffering, and sin are always prominent, while mutual love, tolerance, peace, happiness, and beauty are always fleeting.

so,

People need constant patience to avoid making mistakes or even adding mistakes to them;

People need to be full of kindness to others and other things, to benefit others and other things, so as to resist and dilute the accumulation of evil in life;

People need to be strict with themselves, not to boast, not to be arrogant, not to do shy things, in order to weaken the accumulation of evil in life;

People need to resist the invasion of selfishness and not to seek their own benefits , so that they don't take love as the reason of ignorance and the excuse of asking for it;

People need not to get angry easily, not to calculate the evil of others, so as not to harm others and harm themselves;

People need to not like injustice, but only like the truth, let the justice and the truth guide themselves, and make themselves walk on the right path;

People need to bear all things, believe all things, hope all things, endure all things, let themselves have a broad tolerance, uphold goodness, hope, and be cautious of sin, to treat themselves, others and all things in nature, to create a beautiful future.

The bad influence of original sin on people happens all the time, so the redemption of love should never end.

(2) The true meaning of love

The most typical love is the love between a man and a woman.

"The Lord God said, It is not good for the man to be alone, and I will make him a helper help him.

"...

"The LORD God put him to sleep, and he fell asleep. So he took one of his ribs and closed the flesh.

"So the rib that the LORD God took from the man made a woman and brought her to the man.

"The man said, This is bone of my bones, and flesh of my flesh, and she may be called a woman, because she was taken from a man.

" Therefore a man leaves his father and mother and joins his wife, and the two become one flesh. "

--"Bible"

A woman is a man's "bone in his bones, flesh in his flesh". Man and woman are originally one body. "A man must leave his parents and join his wife, and the two become one body", which is only a return to the original oneness, and this the bridge of unity is love.

Distinguishing the difference between things is the origin of human consciousness and the origin of human "autonomous" life.

Humans perceive and realize based on the "discrimination of the difference between things". Therefore, everything that human beings perceive has a specific nature and is different from external things, so it is not perfect.

And everything in the human world is not perfect, and it needs to be perfect in the changes of time and space. Towards perfection is not only the life course of things, but also the inherent need of things.

Therefore, "love" for "others and other things" means meeting the needs of the other party and making the other party complete with love.

A complete existence is independent of the human world. Therefore, the imperfection of all things in the human world also means the imperfection of man himself. Because the world of people and people is a complete whole, and when people are differentiated from their own world, people and their own world will have a relationship of opposite nature, complementary structure, and interdependence.

Therefore, when the world that a person faces is devastated, the person himself is bound to be bruised and bruised. When a certain need arises in the things in a person's world, the person's own needs will inevitably have corresponding needs.

Therefore, the giving of love is not only "meeting the needs of the other party and making the other person complete because of love", but also "meeting one's own needs and making oneself complete because of love".

In fact, once love is born, it is self who is perfected first. Love will fill up the emptiness, drive away all pain and sin, and fill your life with joy and beauty, and only then will it be passed on to the object of love through the act of love. Because of this, the redemption of love is not only the redemption of others, but also the redemption of oneself, and it is to save oneself first and then save others.

The true meaning of love is that it acts as a bridge that connects two or more imperfect individuals, and makes all connected imperfect individuals perfect because of it.

As the Bible says:

"But speaking the truth in love, in all things grow up into Christ who is the head.

"The whole body is held together by him, each joint according to its function, according to the function of each body, to help each other, so that the body gradually grows and builds itself up in love.

"...

"Dear brothers, we should love one another. For love is from God. Whoever loves is born of God and knows God.

"He who does not love does not know God. For God is love.

"...

"No one has ever seen God. If we love one another, God abides in us, and love for him is perfected in us.

"We know and believe that God loves us. God is love. He who abides in love abides in God, and God abides in him.

"In this way love is perfected in us, so that we may have confidence in the day of judgment. For as he is, so are we in this world.

" There is no fear in love. Perfect love casts out fear. For fear entails punishment. Those who fear are not perfected in love.

"...

"Beyond all this, there is love. Love is the bond of perfection. "

(3) The way of love

"Love does no harm, so love fulfills the law.

"For the whole law is contained in the words 'Love your neighbor as yourself'.

"'You shall love your neighbor as yourself.' There is no greater commandment than these two commandments.

"You shall love one another as I love you, that is my command. "

--"Bible"

Nature has an iron-like law. In the face of this law, all things will prosper if they follow it, and if they go against it, they will perish. In the face of this law, any persistence and obsession of human beings are as light as a feather.

Love fulfills the law, and this law comes from the law of nature and has always followed the law of nature.

Love is to meet the needs of the other party and make the other party complete because of love. Therefore, love is based on meeting the needs of the other person precisely, love is based on obeying the laws of nature, and love is based on the paths of nature. Love does not come only from the catharsis of one's own desires, nor does it only come from the arbitrariness of one's own cognition.

so,

Love fulfills the law without breaking the laws of nature.

Love fulfills the law, so love is sinless.

Love is innocent, so no one has the right to punish love.

Love can't violate the laws of nature, so love may not be right.

Love is not always right, so many people suffer from the heartbreak that comes from love.

Therefore, if a person wants to be innocent and atone for sin, he must love with all his heart. If people want to have a good result, they must follow the laws of nature, take the road of nature as the road, choose the right object, adopt the right ways and methods, and love correctly.

Love does not seek its own benefits. Therefore, love is never an excuse for ignorance, never a reason for seeking. Human needs must follow the paths and laws of nature, and exchange their contributions to nature, all things, and others in exchange for them.

Love is the kindness and benefit to nature, all things, and others. Love is sinless. Love is the atonement for the faults and sins of others. It provides others and others with the way and opportunity to repent, but it cannot guarantee others's repentance of things.

Therefore, only where we love each other is truly sinless.

Therefore, in this world, only by loving each other can we drive out sin, be filled with love, and realize the common well-being of all.

Where is heaven? Where is love, is heaven; where is hell? A place full of sin is hell!

(3) The redemption of love

Humans are originally a part of nature. If they leave nature, they are nothing. If they violate the paths and laws of nature, they can only be hurt.

Since the birth of human beings, they have started the journey of adapting to and following nature. In this process, there are too many people who can't keep up with the footsteps of nature and have experienced tragic lives , and there are too many groups that go against the paths and laws of nature and have been cut off as a whole. However, human beings are still developing and growing step by step through repeated attempts and corrections.

Today, human civilization is highly developed, and human beings have become greedy, cruel, selfish, and conceited in their successes. Too many people and too many groups are obsessed with their own ideas, indulge their own desires, regard ignorance as sacred, and regard shamelessness as freedom .

Love is the core concept of all great thoughts and religions of human beings. However, this era is an era of extreme lack of fraternity and mutual love. People and people, groups of people and groups of people have also become hideous and incompatible with each other.

Love can make people innocent, but it also needs to follow the path and laws of nature, not to mention those sinful ideas, desires, and actions?

Therefore, disasters are coming one by one, and the footsteps of war are getting closer and closer. Humans who do not repent have come to the brink of destruction.

Adapting to nature has enabled mankind to create a splendid civilization; incompatibility with nature has brought human beings to the brink of extinction.

Love needs to follow the laws of nature. Therefore, different types and degrees of love need to choose suitable objects and appropriate methods.

Before the entire human race faces the crisis of extinction, if one people love your own group, let his group inflate and commit sins, his love will also be stained by your own group.

Before the entire human race faced the crisis of extinction, love was not to cater to the obsessions and desires of others, because such love would also be tainted by the object of its own love.

Love itself is sinless, but wrong love will become evil.

Love never ends, so: in this world, as long as a person is not dead, there is a chance for repentance; as long as human beings are not destroyed, there is a possibility of remedy. And all this repentance and remedy can only be based on right love.

6. Sin and Repentance

(1) Women who commit adultery in the Bible

"The scribes and Pharisees came with a woman who had been taken in adultery and made her stand among them.

"And he said to Jesus, "Master, this woman was caught in the act of adultery.

" Moses commanded us in the law to stone such a woman. What do you think should be done to her?"

"When they said this, they tried Jesus to get an accusation against him. But Jesus bent over and wrote on the ground with his finger.

"They kept asking him, and Jesus straightened up and said to them, "Whoever is without sin among you, let him stone her first. "

" So he bent down and wrote on the ground with his fingers.

" When they heard this, they went out one by one, from the old to the young, but Jesus was alone, and the woman was still standing there.

" Jesus straightened up and said to her, "Woman, where are those people?

Has no one condemned you? "

" She said, 'Lord, no. "Jesus said: 'I will not condemn you either, go! Never sin again. '"

--"Bible"

When it comes to fault and sin, tooth for tooth and blood for blood, in fact, is used fault to punish fault, and is used sin to punish sin. Then the human world can only be cycled between fault and sin, and then the human world, from beginning to end, is Only fault and sin.

On the other hand, from a macro point of view, all the real existence in nature is the need of nature, and also has the rationality of its existence. The only difference is that some existences will continue to exist, and some existences will be pruned in the next period.

Therefore, the existence of reality is the result of the selection of nature's history, and it has its own rationality. The selection of nature's history does not represent the future selection of nature, and the rationality of reality also does not represent the rationality of the future.

Therefore, those who are judged as faults and sins by the laws of nature and the laws of the human world will be cut off by nature or human society in the future.

Therefore, any fault or sin in this world has the opportunity to repent, and as long as repentance is in place, it can be accommodated and accepted.

"Jesus said: Do you think these Galileans are more sinful than all the Galileans, and therefore suffer this? I tell you, no! Unless you repent, you will all perish like this!

"Therefore, repent! If you do not repent, I will come to you soon and strike them with the sword of my mouth."

--"Bible"

Faults and sins exist more or less in every individual and every group. Therefore, every individual and every group is moving and changing every moment. The only difference is that some adapt to nature in repentance, so they continue to exist or even grow, while others abandon nature in obsession, so they are pruned or even eliminated.

(2) When a sinner repents, he should rejoice even more

"I tell you this: One sinner who repents is more rejoicing in heaven over him than over ninety-nine righteous who need not repent.

--"Bible"

Compared with small mistakes and small mistakes, complete repentance for major sins is more difficult and more effective. Therefore, each of us should support and rejoice.

7. Confucian ideas of reform

(1) Who has no fault

" Confucius said: "Add me a few years and fifty years to study the "Book of changes", and it will be no big mistake." - "The Analects of Confucius"

The research object of the Book of Changes is the changes of everything in the world (including people) and everything. The Book of Changes originated from Bao Xishi's eight diagrams. Through research, Bao Xishi classified all things in the world (including people) and their changes according to the method of classifying all things with the same attributes. The purpose of making eight diagrams is to communicate with gods, understand the origin of all things in the world, and summarize and classify the changing trends of all things. In Confucius' view, the Book of Changes contains all the truths between heaven and earth.

"When Bao Xishi was king in ancient times, he looked up at the celestial phenomena, looked down at the corresponding changes of everything, looked at the patterns on birds and animals, and looked at the relationship between everything and the geographical environment. According to the shape, change, nature and relationship between himself and everything, he drew eight diagrams, communicated the virtue of gods with eight diagrams, and Classification and representation the shape, change, nature and relationship of everything with eight diagrams.." - "Book of Changes"

"Although the Book of Changes is the abstraction of all things, it contains all the truths of all things." - "Book of Changes "

Confucius said: "Add me a few years and fifty years to study the "Book of changes", and it will be no big mistake. If the saints are like this, what about us ordinary people? This can't help but make people think of this sentence: "Everyone will make mistakes, and being able to correct them is the greatest good."

(2) Don't be afraid to correct mistakes.

Confucius said："If you make a mistake and don't correct it, it's called a mistake. "

Confucius said： " If you make a mistake, don't dare not correct it because of be afraid of being attacked and killed ."

According to Confucius, what is mistake? It is the real fault that one has a fault and does not know how to correct it. People who have a fault should not dare to correct it because they are afraid of being attacked and killed.

The Analects even says that when a villain has a fault, he will inevitably cover up and hide it.

Chinese characters are pictographs. The same Chinese characters and words have different interpretations in different contexts. The root of this lies in the objects and events it refers to.

The distinction between adults and villains in Confucianism can not only describe the difference in size, pattern, and realm of people, but also describe the future direction of people, that is, based on reality, whether the size, pattern, and realm of people will increase or minify.

From the perspective of the former, the present of man is the precipitation of past history, so the reason why a villain is a villain must have the experience and temperament that he has not changed. For people, faults are often revealed, and failure to correct means punishment, so he will inevitably use some means such as covering up and covering up to explain to himself and others in order to pass the test.

From the latter point of view, there is also a contrast between the present and the future. If it can be changed, the size, pattern and realm of people will be relatively larger, and vice versa. People who become smaller are bound to be people who have made mistakes without correcting them. As mentioned above, if you go through without changing, you will inevitably explain to yourself and others by covering up and disguising, so as to muddle through.

There is no medicine for regret in life. Let bygones be bygones. After all, once things happen, there will be no ifs.

There are always opportunities to change in life. If you make a change and start from now, the future will be better.

(3) Let go of the past and face the future

What has already happened, we have no time to change it; what exists now must have a reason for its existence.

People dare not make corrections because they are afraid of being attacked and hurt. In the final analysis, it is still based on the needs of reality and the future.

Sanction what has happened will only create a situation in which each other hurts each other, and will not bring the happiness that everyone wants.

Therefore, in dealing with the past, on the one hand, we must let go of the burden and make corrections when there is a past. On the other hand, we must be lenient and let go of the past.

The Analects of Confucius says: "what has been accomplished, do not lobby or induce; what has already achieved your wish, do not criticize or advise; what has passed, do not pursue or punish."

8. Resolving bad karma in Buddhism

Some people think that the elimination of karma in Buddhism is complete, it is to eliminate all karma, enter the realm of "material and emptiness is not different", finally Nirvana, and achieve positive fruit.

However, "material and emptiness is not different" is the same between the employed and the unemployed, and there is no difference between nirvana and positive results. As discussed in the previous article, "color and space are the same", which is beyond human perception and cannot be described, that is to say, as long as it can be perceived and described, it is not "color and space are the same".

Just like the ultimate perfection, it is everything is exactly the same, everything is no different, and all things are mixed and indistinguishable. It doesn't matter whether there is or isn't, whether it is static or dynamic, whether it is changing or not. For people, it is significant but meaningless.

In the Buddha's world, there is no such thing as having karma or no karma, and there is no such thing as eliminating or not eliminating karma; in the human world, everything is karma, and eliminating karma is crucial.

What kind of karma need to be eliminated, what kind of karma? There is a standard that is "excessive".

Excessive can refer to all behaviors and things that exceed normal limits. It plays a role of kidnapping and destroying itself, the other party and even the whole system .

Confucianism talks about balance", means not being excessive.

The existence of all things requires conditions of balance. Without balance, there will be constant changes.

There is an interdependent relationship between human beings, everything in the world and the natural environment. People's selfishness, which harms others' self-interest, gains a momentary gain and a small profit, but loses the foundation on which they depend for survival.

When people live in the world, they should aim to live better, and if they want to live better, they must maintain the balance required for this better life, they must cherish the heaven and earth, and they must maintain the homeland on which they live.

Therefore, the elimination of karma is to eliminate the karmic karma that kidnaps and destroys oneself, foreign objects, and the system.

9. Repentance of great evil is great goodness，Whoever is full of evil will be punished by the scourge.

(1) The happiness of ordinary people

In a clearing, apple seeds are planted, and an apple tree will grow in the future, and when the apple tree grows, it will bear apples. In the same way, if the seeds of pears were planted at the beginning, they would eventually yield pears; if the seeds of watermelons were planted, they would eventually yield watermelons... What kind of reasons lead to what kind of results, this is a natural law, not at all mysterious.

People can see, hear, smell, feel, and learn the characteristics of things, and use this to organize their thoughts and behaviors according to their own needs. This is humanity.

People will study and work because of their own needs, and exchange the fruits of their labor for the satisfaction of their needs. This is human nature.

Humans can only survive at a suitable temperature, not at extremely low or extremely high temperatures, nor can they fly tens of thousands of miles a day in the blue sky like an airplane. This is the limitation of human beings.

People cannot organize their thoughts and behaviors according to the characteristics of things they have not seen, heard, smelled, felt, or learned. This is also a limitation of human beings.

Buddhism pursues the life realm of truth, goodness and beauty, and many of its contents are beyond the limitations of humanity, humanity and people. For example, the issue of support, because Buddhists' pursuit of a higher realm has gone beyond the scope of humanity and humanity, but his body still belongs to people and needs food, but he can't get food in a humane way like ordinary people, so he needs to enlighten and save ordinary people to get support. For example, the realm that Buddhism can reach and the magical powers that we ordinary people can't reach and possess, because they are beyond the limitations of human beings.Another example is the realm that the great power of Buddhism can reach and the supernatural powers that we can have, which we ordinary people cannot achieve and possess, because they are existences that transcend the limitations of human beings.

Most people live according to their nature, follow the common ways of the world and live within the limitations of others. Plant trees by yourself, reap the consequences, and enjoy yourself. There is no excessive understanding of the true meaning of life and the truth of all things, and there is no excessive contradiction, happiness, pain, merit and evil.

Most people do not have a strong need to transcend human limitations, and they are also restricted by human limitations and obscured by humanity and human nature, and are isolated from the karmic relationship with the Buddhadharma. Just like apple seeds are planted in the fields, pear and watermelon seeds are also planted in the fields, and the managers take care of the pear and watermelon seedlings in every possible way, but let the apple seedlings fend for themselves, or even destroy them deliberately. As you can imagine, Apple is very difficult or even impossible to produce.

Of course, this is not to say that this is not good. On the contrary, this is exactly what Confucianism pursues. The " benevolence " of Confucianism means that people are required to live in humanity, human nature, and their limitations, and that people must work hard to maintain them. Therefore, most people who do not believe in Buddhism can still live happily.

Of course, it's not that it's not good. On the contrary, it's exactly what Confucianism pursues. The Confucian "benevolence" means that people should live in the limitations of humanity, humanity and people, and people should strive to maintain this way of life. Therefore, most people don't believe in Buddhism, but they can live happily.

Although Buddhism pursues the realm of truth, goodness, and beauty, many of its contents are beyond the limitations of humanity, humanity, and human beings, but there are also many contents that fall within the limitations of humanity, humanity, and humans. These contents are "essential and very beneficial "to the happiness of life. This is also the reason why offerings can be realized in the human world.

(2) The relationship between the great good and the great evil and Buddhism

The most typical example is the relationship between the great good and the great evil and Buddhism.

People with great goodness have lofty goals in life, have a firm disposition, are full of joy, are brave and diligent, and become sanctified and become Buddhas in favorable circumstances.

A person who has the fate of great evil is a person who is full of evil, but has not completely lost his conscience and can turn back in the bitter sea.

A person who has a relationship with great evil is a person who is full of evil, but has not completely lost his conscience, and can turn back in the sea of suffering.

Mr. Jin Yong's novels have a wonderful description in this regard.

"The Sweeping Monk" has a wonderful discussion on martial arts and Buddhism: "There are seventy-two stunts in this temple, each of which can hurt people's vital points and kill people. It is necessary to have the corresponding compassionate Buddhism to resolve it. This principle is not well known to the monks in this monastery, but after one person has practiced four or five stunts, his understanding of Zen will naturally be hindered. In my Shaolin school , then it is called 'Martial Learning Obstruction', which is the same as the 'knowledge and seeing obstacles' of other sects and schools. It should be noted that Buddhism seeks to save the world, and martial arts is to kill, and the two run counter to each other. Only the higher the Buddha, the more compassionate The more prosperous, the better the martial arts skills can be practiced, but the eminent monks who have reached such a state of cultivation are disdainful to learn all kinds of powerful killing methods . "

In Mr. Jin Yong's novels: "Jiu Mozhi" and "Xie Xun" have done a lot of big mistakes, and they all endured great pain afterward. They finally realized Buddhism and became a generation of eminent monks; while " Cheng Kun" and "Li Xun" " Mo Chou " is paranoid about love and hatred, falls into the devil's way and cannot repent, and eventually dies of misfortune.

Although the plots of Mr. Jin Yong's novels are fictitious, their rationale is thorough and profound, which can be used for reference.

Just as "Jiu Mozhi" and "Xie Xun" can eventually become a generation of eminent monks, the progress of the practice of evil karma is not slow at all, the difference is that the process is accompanied by huge suffering.

(3) The Story of King Ajatasa

In the history of Buddhism, there was a King Ajatasatra who killed his parents, usurped power and seized the throne, opposed the Buddha, and committed five serious crimes. .

"For those who are resurrection after death in the top grade, there is no need to accept, uphold, read and recite the prescriptions and other classics. Be good at interpreting the meaning and interest, in the first meaning, not disturbed, deeply believe in cause and effect, and not slander the Mahayana. With this merit, I wish to live in bliss. "

- "Buddha's Commentary on Infinite Longevity"

Being resurrection after death in the middle of the top grade is very rare in Buddhism, and it requires a lot of wisdom and sincerity. But we know that King Ajatasattva is a wicked man, and he repented to the Buddha because he was afraid of going to hell. Can his wisdom and sincerity reach the standard of a high-grade middle-born? What about the sins he had committed in the past? Why did he go to the bliss of rebirth, or was he still a middle-ranked student?

The answer is merit.

He is notorious, his repentance, his rebirth in Pure Land, and the possessor has a powerful educational effect, which can lead more people to repent and repent.

As a king, he has supreme power. His repentance and repentance have a strong supporting effect on Buddhism and Dharma.

The repentance and repentance of the great wicked will turn the great sin into great merit, so after repentance, the wicked man becomes a good man.

If King Ajatasatra had not repented and repented, he would have fallen into the Avici Hell as his final destination, so he was full of evil and would be punished by heaven.

Nature is fair. No matter how much sin people have done, they need to use much merit to atone for their sins, so that they won't be punished for their sins.

Therefore, people with great wickedness should see the two prospects of "the benefits of repentance and the consequences of being stubborn" and repent; society and the people should tolerate their repentance and create conditions for their repentance, and at the same time they should maintain the natural path and rules, maintain the normal order of human society, and punish those who are obsessive.

10. Don't let sin continue to hurt yourself

The human nervous system is bounded by the human body and does not exist beyond the human body. The existence and changes of the outside world are perceived by acting on the nervous system. Different external changes and their processes correspond to the process of the changes and changes of different nervous systems.

The result of people's cognition of all things in the outside world comes from and is reflected in the human nervous system, and The result of people's cognition of all things in the outside world comes from and is reflected in the human body too.

The interaction between people and things outside, the result is the movement and changes of people and things. Movement changes not only reflect the relative changes of people and foreign objects, but also reflect the changes of people and foreign objects relative to their original state. This kind of change is the reflection and precipitation of the interaction process on people and foreign objects.

Therefore, a person has gone through bad, sad, resentful... and other bad processes, which will eventually leave precipitation on oneself and external objects (including others). After the process is over, It is the precipitation left in oneself that can make oneself experience hurt again.

example: two children fought and were taken home by their respective adults. One of the children was crying all the time. In fact, the fight was over, and it was the injury left on him that made him cry. The next day, the two children fought again and were led home by their respective adults again. The child cried even harder, and this time, what made him cry was the superposition of the two injuries left on him.

No matter what a person has experienced, he should quickly smooth the wound, leave himself peaceful and comfortable, and don't let the hurt that settles in himself continue to hurt himself.

No matter what a person has experienced, he should stand outside himself and the process, look at this experience, let himself understand the physics and human feelings, and make himself better at success and better at getting auspicious and comfortable.

When two children fight, no matter who wins or loses, it is both sides who are malicious. The essence of right and wrong, right and evil, aggression and defense is to put each other in a hostile position.

Sunrise and moonset, which is right or wrong? Cows and sheep eat grass, who is right and who is wrong? In nature, there is only the interaction of all things and their movement changes. Good and evil, right and wrong, right and wrong are all human obsessiveness (recognized is group obsessiveness).

Too often, both sides of the enemy think that they are good, right, and right. Knowing mistakes and making mistakes is only rooted in the damage accumulated in oneself, and this damage is brought up by oneself little by little, step by step.

How much malice there is, there is how much damage is accumulated; the degree of sin reflects the depth and breadth of the damage in oneself.

Good corresponds to peace, comfort and health, and evil corresponds to crisis and harm to the sick.

Kindness is never one's kindness to the outside world, but an expression of one's own serenity, comfort and health.

So, being kind to everything is actually being kind to yourself.

CHAPTER 4: AWAKENING HUMAN CONSCIOUSNESS

1.he predicament of the times

Industrialization has greatly enriched people's material life. The quality of our material life is higher than that of ancient kings and emperors.

We eat things that the ancients could not eat, and use things that the ancients have never seen before. Our world is far more exciting than the ancients' world.

However, we demand far more from nature than the ancients, and our destruction of the ecological environment is far more severe than that of the ancients.

So, we face an unprecedented punishment from nature.

In recent years, forest fires, locust plagues, extreme high temperatures, heavy rainstorms, the new coronavirus... One disaster after another has made life in this world utterly devastated. What is even more terrifying is climate change, melting glaciers, rising sea levels, ancient viruses, Yellowstone volcanoes... These foreseeable or possible larger disasters are approaching us step by step.

In the face of nature's punishment, the probability of human extinction is rising.

The most terrifying thing is the strong and stubborn self-awareness of every country, every nation and every organization in the world today.

People are kidnapped into their own countries, nations, and organizations, and they are engaged in fierce, even life-and-death struggles in the ideological, economic, political, and even military fields.

In economic struggle, the most important thing is to develop one's own economy. Everyone's crazy economic development will inevitably lead to the demand for nature and the aggravation of the damage to the ecological environment.

Political struggles revolve around the interests of groups, sever the natural connection between nature and human beings, violate the way of heaven and humanity, destroy the proper order of human society, and plunge human society into a whirlpool of selfishness, greed, and cruelty.

In military struggle, one kills one thousand enemies and one loses eight hundred, and there is no winner. It is kill each other within the human race, and it is a crime committed by people against the same kind. With the current level of weapons, especially the existence of a large number of nuclear weapons, a large-scale military struggle may mean the destruction of mankind.

The military struggle will produce a lot of damage and consumption, and these will lead to the demand for nature and the aggravation of the damage to the ecological environment. As an old Chinese saying goes: After the soldiers, there will be a year of disaster.

Natural disasters will not only cause disasters to people, but also cause difficulties on a broader level, and these difficulties will intensify the struggle between people.

The mutual causation and interweaving of natural and man-made disasters is a sad portrayal of our era.

2. The natural conditions and basis for the awakening of human consciousness

(1) People are the most basic and natural characteristics of oneself

The genetic similarity between humans and humans is as high as 99.99%, and there is reproductive isolation between humans and animals. This shows that no matter what country, ethnicity, or religious belief, first of all, a person is a person, and people are our most basic and natural characteristics.

Americans, Germans, Chinese, Russians, Iranians, Namibians... No matter what country you are, first of all, a person is a person, and people are our most basic and natural characteristics; Chinese, Brazilians, Germans, Arabs People, French people... No matter what nationality you are, first of all, a person is a person, and people are our most basic and natural characteristics; Christians, Buddhists, Muslims, Hindus... No matter what religion you are, first of all, a person is a person, and people are our most basic and natural characteristics.

The highly similar material structure between people determines the highly similar cognition and behavior between people. Therefore, there are a lot of similarities between different cultural systems, and different languages can translate and communicate with each other.

Apple, people in different countries call it different, but everyone feels the same about it; Love is the common advocacy of all the great ideas and religions that can last forever in the world, and its connotation in different thought and religious systems is also the same in a large amount.

After all, we are all human beings.

(2) The fundamental difference between man and all things

Many people think that human beings are different from all things because human beings have subjective consciousness, but this is not the case. In fact, animals basically have subjective consciousness, because they will actively hunt down their prey, they will avoid disasters, and they will build nests (part of them)... Even many animals have the ability to learn and think. These phenomena show that they have self-awareness and can also take active actions based on their survival needs. Therefore, it is unrealistic to say that only human beings have subjective consciousness.

Compared with the nervous system of animals, there is no essential difference between the human nervous system and the animal nervous system, except that it is more precise and more complex. The awakening of human consciousness comes from the precipitation of historical actions (the historical precipitation of interaction with foreign objects), and of course the consciousness of animals also comes from this precipitation, because from the perspective of evolution, humans and animals originated from an ancestor, and the Differentiation results from differences in historical as (historical interaction with foreign objects). Therefore, the difference in the precision and complexity of the nervous system is the fundamental difference in consciousness between humans and animals.

We can imagine that if a baby is allowed to live in the wild after birth on the premise of ensuring its safety, and only given necessary food aid (food aid is cut off after it has certain predation ability), what will such a person look like in adulthood? He can't speak or think in a normal way, because he doesn't live in human society, he won't enjoy the guidance of human society for his actions (including thinking and doing), and his way of life will be very different from that of normal people. However, he has the human nervous system, which is the natural ability of a person, so he is smarter than other animals and better at learning new abilities to meet his own survival needs. That's all, he can't even be stronger than a chimpanzee's survival ability, because chimpanzees enjoy the guidance of the population's actions (including thinking and doing). In addition, human civilization has basically separated people from the wild survival, while chimpanzees have been living in the wild all the time, and chimpanzees are naturally more suitable for the wild survival than he is.

Such a person no longer has the conditions to be a person.

Therefore, the fundamental reason why a person can be distinguished from other animals is that he was born as a human (inherited human genes) and grew up in human society (enjoyed the guidance of human society).

(3) Without a self of the same kind, you are nothing

Life comes from parents, parents have parents, and human genes are passed down from generation to generation. Nature has nurtured all things, and all things have their own forms. Without parents and grandparents, human beings would not have human genes and forms, that is, human material structure.

Let us take the blue sky as an example to illustrate the effect of material structure on people.

Science tells people that the blue sky is a picture created by atmospheric molecules, ice crystals, water droplets and sunlight. When sunlight enters the atmosphere, colored light with long wavelength, such as red light, has great transmission power and can penetrate the atmosphere to the ground. However, the violet, blue and cyan light with short wavelength is prone to scattering when encountering atmospheric molecules, ice crystals, water droplets, etc. The scattered violet, blue and cyan light fills the sky, making the sky blue.

In fact, according to scientific theory, people see that the sky is blue, and it is also related to the human visual system. The human visual system allows people to perceive red, orange, yellow, green, blue, blue, and purple, and the different colors of light allow us to see and distinguish them. Blue sky. Just imagine, if the human visual system only allows people to perceive violet light in the wavelength range of 390~435 nanometers, the sky that people see is definitely a purple sky, and the human world becomes only pitch black or purple.

Further, if there is no visual system that can perceive visible light similar to that of human beings in the world, then the so-called blue sky does not exist. On the contrary, there are no atmospheric molecules, ice crystals, water droplets, etc. co-created with sunlight, or the characteristics of both have enough scale changes, even if there are more visual systems like mine, you won't see the blue sky.

Therefore, the blue sky is the co-creation of atmospheric molecules, ice crystals, water droplets, sunlight and me under certain conditions, instead of having a blue sky there.

"Atmospheric molecules, ice crystals, water droplets, sunlight, and people" have their own characteristics, which are our respective karma. "Atmospheric molecules, ice crystals, water droplets, sunlight, and people" create the "Blue Sky".

In other words, the blue sky is the result of the "karmic origin" of the three, and by extension, the world in front of people is the result of the "karmic origin" between humans and external objects.

Just like the "baby born in the wild" above, leaving human society, his life can only be simulated with animals.

another example, let's imagine that when mankind perishes, there is only a normal adult left in the world: he can speak, but he has no object to communicate with, so the so-called speaking loses its meaning; he has His own language, there is a lot of knowledge to learn, but it can only be done within the scope of his understanding, and those that he does not understand are useless because of lack of support; he has a lot of tools and resources, but all the Everything needs to be done by himself, so he can only use those related to his own needs, because without support, the others are useless after all...

In the face of the pressure of survival, he must abandon a large number of human thoughts, life, and survival patterns, and live more and more like an animal. If he lives long enough, he will lose all human survival patterns.

In a word, without the same self, you are nothing.

3. Awakening the consciousness of the human race

(1) Human consciousness and human world

The exploration of the true state of nature is a question raised by man to himself, and the result is bound to be beyond the scope of man's cognition.

People touch themselves and the outside world with their eyes, ears, nose, tongue, body and consciousness, and realize the changes of themselves and the outside world with consciousness. The result of feeling is change, and the change produces consciousness (or non-conscious coping, such as conditioned reflex). People's cognition of the real situation of nature is the result of this feeling and consciousness. People can't know what they can't feel and realize.

The object of human awakening is change, and the premise of change is different; people cannot be awakened to two or more changes at the same time, and awakening is manifested as a process of change. Therefore, human cognition must begin to distinguish the difference and carry out a process of change.

Without the difference in appearance, the sequence of time, the difference in spatial position, and the process of movement change, it is impossible for people to recognize. Therefore, the appearance, time, and space of existence are only ways of human cognition, but they may not be the truth of nature.

The process of people distinguishing things is accompanied by the collection of situations and attributes. When people distinguish themselves from foreign things, they will find that there is a causal relationship between themselves and foreign things. It is their own feelings about foreign things that lead to changes that can produce consciousness. This change is the result of causal relationship between themselves and foreign things. Things that have no causal relationship with themselves can't lead to changes that make people realize, so they can't be realized or recognized.

Science and technology have greatly expanded people's cognitive ability, but science and technology actually started from expanding people's ability to feel things. Scientific instruments and methods expand the range of people's feelings about things. No matter how big the scope is and how long the path is, it must eventually lead to changes that can make people conscious through causality, and then people can produce cognition.

Therefore, no matter how advanced science and technology are, people can only recognize things that have causal relationship with their own world.

Even if there is a thing around people or even inside people's bodies, as long as it can't lead to changes that can make people realize, people can't recognize it. No matter how far and how different a thing is from people, it can be recognized as long as it has a causal relationship (whether direct or indirect) with changes that can make people realize.

Therefore, the world that people can recognize must be a world in which everything is causally related to each other, but the causal relationship between all things is not necessarily a natural reality. Because such a world is based on people's distinction of things, and the collection of conditions and attributes of things, and this foundation itself is artificial and may also be wrong.

(2) The production of subjective consciousness and its illusory nature

Every act of man in the world (including thinking and doing) will cause more or less changes in the elements of the system related to this act. The accumulation of such changes over time will strengthen some aspects of people's thinking, behavior and even the structure of human life, while others will weaken or even eliminate them.

Different intensities and different times of accumulation have different degrees of accumulation in one existence . For existences with a high degree of accumulation, the lower the threshold for obtaining resources and channels, the easier it is to be called by the system. When the current period reaches a certain level, they will have a chain reaction with normal perception and behavioral activities. It will pop out automatically. For example: conditioned reflex.

This is also one of the sources of misunderstanding and wrong response.

Humans are involved in every action that interacts with all things, so every action of human beings strengthens my concept. This is also the reason why it is most difficult for practitioners to get rid of "ego".

Subjective consciousness is the result of this kind of accumulation. Because it is highly accumulated, it always appears in people's perception. Today, when science has been relatively highly developed, it is easy for people to find that through the interaction between existence, existence can be realized. To explain it by the change of motion, it just can't find its existence.

Subjective consciousness arises from this cumulative process and is the result of the interaction between the human nervous system and the outside world. Fundamentally speaking, there is no subjective consciousness, everything is natural, everything comes naturally.

(3) The important role of subjective consciousness

Subjective consciousness is The interaction between the nervous system of that part of people and the outside world which is being constantly strengthened and always jumps out in people's life activities. Subjective consciousness is of great significance to people's life and life activities.

Subjective consciousness will participate in all conscious life activities of human beings, and it will interact and influence with these life activities of human beings, thus forming a larger and more complex interaction system.

In this process, subjective consciousness will always maintain its influence on people's life activities, and even it will consciously lead people's life activities, so as to achieve people's life goals.

When people are very hungry, their subjective consciousness will lead them to get food to eat; when their hands are injured, their subjective consciousness will lead them to do all the actions needed for healing; when experience and reason tell people that something is wrong and dangerous Yes, subjective consciousness will control people's impulse to want to do, to do...

With the development of human civilization, people's needs are more diversified, people's life activities are more complicated, more and more things need to be handled correctly by people, and the unconscious stress response is far from meeting people's survival needs. The role of subjective consciousness becomes more and more important.

Subjective consciousness, especially the subjective consciousness that has experienced the baptism of human civilization, can make people better follow the natural path and rules, better adapt to the natural ecological environment, and better perform the mission given to them by nature.

The important role of subjective consciousness is also reflected in its life care.

Subjective consciousness arises from people themselves, and its driving force is also the needs of people's own life activities. Therefore, it has always played an important role in meeting people's needs, maintaining people's survival and interests, and realizing people's life goals.

(4) Limitations of Subjective Consciousness

Subjective consciousness arises from people themselves, and its driving force is also the needs of people's own life activities. Therefore, it is inherently selfish and objectively greedy, so it is possible to do evil.

To say it is selfish is because the subjective consciousness is limited to oneself and is driven by one's own needs. It is naturally unable to understand the needs of others and other things, and it can only indirectly cause people's perception and awareness through interaction with people. After the needs of others and other things are perceived and awakened, if they cannot be combined with their own needs, they will lose the driving force to satisfy them, and people will not do anything.

It is greedy because the driving force of subjective consciousness is people's own needs. As long as there is this demand, it will have the driving force. The actions of people led by it naturally fail to take into account the limits of natural and social actions towards people. If without external constraints, it is easy to break through this limit.

When the subjective consciousness and the actions of the people it leads do not follow the natural path and rules, nor the social morals and norms, and bring adverse effects or even disasters to others, society, and nature, it is doing evil.

People rely on their eyes, ears, nose, tongue, body, and consciousness to feel themselves and the outside world, and rely on consciousness to realize the changes in themselves and the outside world. The result of feeling is change, and the change produces awareness.

The changes that people realize are changes in themselves, and it can even be said as changes in the human nervous system.

Therefore, people's subjective consciousness will lose its reflection on the real situation of the world because of its unreasonable temperament and desire. People's subjective consciousness will lose the reflection of the real situation of the world because of the change of their own and the outside world's subjective consciousness conditions. People's subjective consciousness will produce a false reflection of the real situation of the world due to unreasonable and deceptive stimuli from the outside world.

Therefore, the subjective consciousness has the possibility of distorted reflection of the real situation of the world, and this distortion will cause a series of mistakes, even sins, in the actions of people dominated by the subjective consciousness.

Therefore, the actions of people dominated by subjective consciousness may not conform to the natural path and rules, and may not be feasible in reality.

One person thinks it is right, and everyone thinks it is right. It is be feasible in the reality.

Individuals think it is right, not everyone thinks it is right. Everyone thinks it is right, but it may not be feasible in the reality.

Individuals think it is right, not everyone thinks it is right. Everyone thinks it is right, but it may not be feasible in reality.

If a person thinks it is right and everyone thinks it is wrong, he will encounter many difficulties in society.

One person thinks it is right, and everyone thinks it is right, but it is not feasible in reality. It is of no use at all.

(5) The evil of national consciousness

As mentioned above: in the face of the punishment of nature, the probability of human extinction is rising. What is even more impressive is the strong and stubborn self-awareness of every country, nation, and organization in the world today. People have been kidnapped into their own country, nation, and organization, and are engaged in intense ideological, economic, political, and even military affairs. or even a life-and-death struggle . The mutual causation and interweaving of natural and man-made disasters is a sad portrayal of our era.

Among all the strong and stubborn self-consciousness, the national consciousness is the most terrible, because the current human society divides people, ideology, culture, economy, politics and military affairs on the basis of the state. Although universal values and globalization dilute this division, it is still deeply rooted, especially the military division, which has become one of the possibilities for the total destruction of mankind.

Due to the stubborn national consciousness, when human beings face global natural disasters, although everyone knows what to do, because of their own national interests, they cannot reach a consensus and waste the opportunity of human self-redemption.

On August 9, the UN IPCC report "Climate Change 2021: A Natural Science Basis" was released. Unlike previous assessments, the IPCC report officially confirms that humans are to blame for climate change. Scientists warned in the report: The rate of global warming is faster than expected, and if no action is taken, the disaster facing mankind will be inevitable.

On November 1, speaking at the World Leaders Summit of the 26th Conference of the Parties to the United Nations Framework Convention on Climate Change, he said: "Humanity has come to a critical juncture, and the risk of a sharp escalation of global warming and a vicious circle is imminent. But A virtuous circle of sustainable growth, job creation and opportunity can be created as long as there is increased investment in a net-zero emissions and climate-resilient economic model. He urged global leaders to be ambitious and united to protect our future, save mankind"

It is still unknown what countries will do after this summit, as well as the fate of mankind.

The fact that human beings can get to where they are today is entirely at the hands of the stubborn self-consciousness of various countries. All countries want to gain more benefits and take less responsibility. They are all watching and comparing. As long as there is a group of black sheep, Make the whole world doomed.

Up to now, the new crown epidemic has infected nearly 250 million people and claimed more than 5 million lives. It has brought huge losses and difficulties to the world economy. However, the issue of tracing the origin of the epidemic continues to be beaten between countries.

In addition to the above-mentioned disasters, many disasters have occurred around the world this year. However, under the global disaster, at the threshold of human life and death, the selfishness, greed, brutality and irrationality of the national consciousness have been revealed. The world is full of struggles between countries and the pace of war. also getting closer.

The mutual causation and interweaving of natural and man-made disasters is a sad portrayal of our era.

No matter whether the human beings in the future are destroyed by natural disasters or nuclear wars, the stubborn national consciousness is to blame!

In this era when national consciousness has become the biggest driver of human demise, weakening national consciousness has become a major issue for all mankind.

As the saying goes: the rise and fall of the world is the responsibility of every man. In this era of severe disasters, in this era when national consciousness has become the biggest obstacle to human self-help, a person who loves his own country is doing evil!

Patriotism is equal to evil, which is the inevitable result of the over-expanded national consciousness; patriotism, etc. and evil are issues that everyone should be aware of.

Note: This chapter was written several months ago. At present, the Russian-Ukrainian war has attracted the attention of the whole world, and almost no one has paid attention to the issue of climate change. However, climate change is still intensifying, its threat to the whole mankind is also increasing, and the prospect of human destruction is becoming more and more obvious.

(6) Awakening the consciousness of the human race

Subjective consciousness plays an important role in meeting people's needs, maintaining people's survival and interests, and realizing people's life goals.

Natural disasters and the threat of war have pushed mankind to the brink of extinction, providing a need and opportunity for the awakening of the consciousness of the human race.

Human is the most basic and natural characteristic of every human being, and it provides the conditions and the way for the awakening of human consciousness.

Awakening the consciousness of the human race, for everyone, the first thing is to walk the way of heaven and the way of human beings. Respond to the needs of nature, fulfill the mission entrusted to you by nature, follow the paths and rules of nature, and exchange your own contributions to nature and others for your own needs.

Awakening the consciousness of the human race, for each person, defines himself with the most basic characteristics endowed by nature. Dilute the consciousness of one's own group, organization, race, and country, strengthen one's own consciousness of the human race, strive for the survival and common interests of mankind, and live in harmony with others within the framework of the entire human race, and do not discriminate against, be hostile to or hurt others under the abduction of the consciousness of groups, organizations, races and countries.

Awakening the consciousness of the Terran, for the society, the first thing is to fear nature and obey the natural road and rules. We should respect science, the most effective means for human beings to know nature at present, so that scientific ideas, methods and conclusions can effectively guide people to deal with major problems of human society; We should safeguard our naturally formed human values and way of life. Naturally formed values refer to equality, freedom, democracy, competition, diversity, love, tolerance and repentance, etc. The natural way of life means that people respond to the needs of nature, fulfill the mission entrusted to them by nature, follow the roads and rules of nature, and exchange their contributions to nature and other things for their own needs.

Awakening the consciousness of the Terran is to establish and strengthen the concept and mechanism of the Terran for the society. The whole human society should establish and strengthen a concept and mechanism to safeguard the survival and interests of the human society, maintain the normal social order of the human society, and safeguard everyone's rights and interests fairly and justly, and weaken the consciousness and unity of isolated, stubborn, selfish, greedy and cruel groups, organizations, races and countries in the human society.

In this time of disaster and disaster, at the intersection of human life and death, human beings can realize self-redemption only by awakening the consciousness of the human race.

(7) The expansion of the powers of the United Nations

In the face of nature's punishment, the probability of human extinction is rising. What is even more impressive is the strong and stubborn self-awareness of every country, nation, and organization in the world today. People have been kidnapped into their own country, nation, and organization, and are engaged in intense ideological, economic, political, and even military affairs , or even a life-and-death struggle. The mutual causation and interweaving of natural and man-made disasters is a sad portrayal of our era.

The expansion of the powers of the United Nations is an effective measure to resolve the strong and stubborn national consciousness and the bottomless international struggle.

At the same time, the awakened consciousness of the human race also needs the expansion of the power of the United Nations to execute its own will. Because there is only the awakening of the consciousness of the human race, and the human being without the expansion of the power of the United Nations is just a vegetative person.

The expansion of the powers of the United Nations is a major event for the entire human race. It requires the participation of all people, and it is necessary to design perfect systems and mechanisms to enable human beings to effectively respond to crises and to enable human beings to survive and prosper for a long time.

This article only presents a few superficial ideas, in order to attract more ideas.

First, natural paths and rules

Human society, in order to survive and grow for a long time, needs to constantly change itself and adapt to the paths and rules of nature.

In this world, nothing is closer to the laws and trends of nature than science, and no one is closer to justice than scientists.

Note: There are laws and trends in the road, and the rules are put forward to highlight the importance of people obeying the rules.

Therefore, the expansion of the powers of the United Nations requires scientific guidance and the participation of scientists, so that the decision-making and behavior of the human race can be more adapted to the roads and rules of nature, so as to ensure the survival and development of the human race.

If scientists only have the power to make suggestions and appeals, and can't go deep into the decision-making process of human beings, then the political and decision-making process of human beings can only be a contest and wrangling between "organizations and organizations" or "countries and countries" based on strength, interests and obligations.

When justice and science give way to strength and interests, the final result is that human beings cannot find the way to self-redemption.

Of course, scientists who participate in the human decision-making process must be pure scientists, without any entanglement of interests related to participating events, and they need to accept the most extensive social supervision.

Second, maintain the human values and way of life derived from nature

Values derived from nature such as equality, freedom, democracy, competition, diversity, love, tolerance and repentance, etc; the way of life derived from nature means that people respond to the needs of nature, fulfill the mission entrusted to them by nature, and obey the The way and rules of nature, in exchange for one's own needs for one's own contribution to nature and others.

To maintain the human values and way of life derived from nature is to form a mechanism to maintain such human values and way of life, and to form a restrictive mechanism for violating such values and way of life.

For example, forming a restriction mechanism for behaviors rooted in selfish and greedy national interests, such as sophistry, evading responsibility and seeking illegitimate interests; Form a restriction mechanism to disrupt the normal order of the Terran, such as moral kidnapping, interest kidnapping, forced trading, and interest collusion (especially the behavior of soliciting votes through interest transmission is the worst).

The more in times of crisis, the more we must maintain the human values and way of life that come from nature.

Local disasters, for the people directly affected by the disaster, are life and death, but for the whole human race, the normal supply and demand chain is cut off.

Human society is already a society with a highly developed social division of labor. To survive, everyone needs to use the fruits of their labor and a large number of others to exchange what they need . A person's chain of existence is related to many people, and the people he is related to are related in this way。 Continue to expand, it is the interconnection of all people in the whole world.

When the disaster cuts off the supply and demand chain, especially the key supply and demand chain, a series of reactions will occur, resulting in the unmet needs of a large number of people, which will cause the society to lose its normal order, and then lead to a large number of evils. The causal and intertwining of natural and man-made disasters began.

Therefore, the more in times of crisis, the more we must maintain the human values and way of life that come from nature.

Of course, when a serious disaster occurs, the above alone is not enough to deal with it. At this time, it is necessary to activate the redemption mechanism of human beings - love.

Love is not seeking its own benefits, sympathizing with the suffering of others, meeting the needs of others, bridging the breakpoints in the chain of supply and demand, in order to maintain human "values and ways" of that come from nature, and in order to avoid larger and wider disasters.

In a normal society, when disaster strikes, it will guide, inspire, and encourage love in people's hearts, and rely on people's mutual love to achieve redemption. Instead of being indifferent, holding resources tight, narrowing the pattern, and letting the supply and demand chain break, resulting in the mutual causal and intertwined results of natural and man-made disasters.

In disasters, love is the embodiment of responsibility, and self-preservation is the root of sin.

Third, abolish the one-vote veto power of the five permanent members of the Security Council

The US-Soviet hegemony has formed two major camps in the world. The Cold War has finally ended, but the competition between the US, China and Russia has made the world even more dangerous.

We can see that the leaders of the two opposing sides are often one of the five permanent members. It is precisely because of their veto power that the United Nations can't form an effective resolution to resolve disputes, which makes the United Nations useless and can only watch them fight endlessly.

We have seen that because of the veto power, the five permanent members can protect their illegitimate interests and actions, and even protect the illegitimate interests and actions of other countries through the veto power of a certain country. This destroys the human values and way of that come from nature, and makes human beings lose the ability to promote good and abandon evil.

Without a resolution that can effectively resolve disputes, justice will not be revealed, the actions to safeguard justice will lose its legitimacy, justice will be overwhelmed by national interests and the world will lose its normal order.

Therefore, abolishing the one-vote veto power of the five permanent members of the Security Council is the only way for the UN to expand its powers, and it is also the only way to maintain justice and order in the international community.

Fourth, oppose a monopoly in any field

For society, Monopoly in any field is a cancer. Ideological autocracy, economic monopoly, political dictatorship, military hegemony, etc, are all cancers.

Awakening the consciousness of the human race and expanding the power of the United Nations is to unite mankind to deal with the current disasters and dilemmas, to safeguard the human values and way of life that come from nature, and to ensure the long-term existence and prosperity of mankind.

Therefore, human beings must not be allowed to fall into despotism or dictatorship in a certain field, or even despotism and dictatorship in all fields, so that human society loses its vitality, and the entire human race falls into a situation of enslavement and suffering that cannot be saved.

This is a very important subject that requires the participation of all human beings to form a comprehensive and powerful restraining mechanism.

4. Abandon Communism

(1) Ideal and reality

"A specter, the specter of communism, wandering in Europe," opened Pandora's Box, triggered catastrophe in human history, and brought innumerable evils.

Perhaps, Marx and Engels did not expect that under the guidance of the theory of communism, all the communist countries will all trades is declining, and people will be starving for cruel and bottomless struggles, which will become a hell on earth; All countries have become associated with dictatorships and become rogue countries, exporting evil everywhere in the world; all communist countries have used their sinful and tragic histories to prove that this road is not feasible!

The ideal described by communism is beautiful, and we can also believe that Marx and Engels have noble morals and lofty sentiments, but this theory is too immature, contrary to the laws and trends of nature, and destroys the normal regulations and Order of human society , ignoring people's innate disposition, the result can only be counterproductive.

Communism, rebelling against Heaven, destroying order, and distorting human nature, is the root of all evil, and is a devil wearing an angel mask.

(2) Reason and human nature

Human feet follow the way. Evil theories have created an evil system, an evil system, blocking the path of goodness, dredging the path of evil, allowing the good to be rewarded for evil, and the evil to be rewarded for good.

The human heart is guided by reason. The theory of evil makes goodness turn into evil, legalize evil, makes people betray by their relatives with kindness, and makes evil people full of sense of justice.

The driving force of people's behavior is their own needs, and people will naturally follow the path that can satisfy their own needs; The way of people's thoughts is reason. With theory that can dredge people's emotions, people will naturally be full of sense of justice.

Therefore, people who do evil do not have a bad nature, nor are they unable to distinguish between good and evil. They are just theories of evil that go against the way of heaven, reverse black and white, and distort human nature.

Evil was not originally terrible, but what was terrible was that evil always succeeded; sin was not originally terrible, but what was terrible was the reasonableness and legality of sin.

People who do evil often have more reasons than those who do good. Knowing that he may be wrong, he is more motivated to look for various reasons to make himself feel at ease and confident, and he is also more motivated to find more reasons to prove that his actions are correct and must be successful, they deceive themselves and others in this way.

The history of the world, the history of China, has fully proved that communism is evil and unworkable, but why are there still a small group of people who insist on this theory and are forcing the Chinese people to adhere to this theory?

Because this theory protects their interests and gives them a reason to deceive themselves; because they are afraid of ending this theory, they will not only lose their vested interests, but also be judged justly!

Evil theories are bound to marry evil, and even if they are at the end of their lives, they will still be together and struggle to the death!

Before dawn is the darkest moment, evil ways, the more at the end of the road, the more serious sins will be brought!

The theory of goodness and beauty conform to the laws and trends of nature, conform to the disposition and well-being of all living beings, maintain the justice and order of the human world, dispel evil in the human world, and bring light and auspiciousness to all living beings.

What this world needs is good and beautiful theory , not wicked theory!

(3) The transmission of sin

Theory can dredge people's emotions and make people justified. In the process of social practice, the connotation of theory will continue to be enriched, refined, and extended vertically, and it will even break through the original boundaries in many aspects.

The theory says that should, can, must will slowly appear in the chain of practice; the theory says that to seize, in the chain of practice, cruel murder will gradually appear. The countless havoc and the countless evils may not be the original intention of Marx and Engels, but it is a real effect.

In the process of social practice, theory often "a small mistake will lead to a great sin", or even produces the opposite result.

Christianity teaches people that "If someone hits you on the right cheek, even the left cheek will be turned around by him." Such a pure and good doctrine has also made mistakes in the process of social practice; Buddhism teaches people with truth, goodness and beauty, and resolve first save all beings and then become Buddha yourself, but it also drags down the society in the process of social practice; Confucianism advocates harmonious coexistence between man and nature, and between man and man, but it also leads to tragedy in the process of social practice...

These doctrines and ideas of perfection and perfection have even been deviated in the process of social practice, not to mention the communism that goes against heaven, destroys order, distorts human nature, and promotes violence?

(4) Costs and achievements

There has never been a result in this world, without a cause. The evils of a society are rampant, a group of people is in dire straits. The small group of mischievous aliens, and the gang of eagle dogs in captivity are not the main reasons. Those who "endured silently in suffering, obeyed and succumbed under obscenity, and dared not dare" are the main reasons. Because they cannot maintain the Road of Heaven and humanity. Because they cannot maintain social justice and order. Because they cannot protect their reasonable interests and power.

The Bible says, "Whoever is without sin among you, let him be the first to stone her. "

Those who are wicked will turn their backs into good ones, and they will create even greater merits!

Fighting violence with violence, eradicating evil with evil, killing one thousand enemies and self-defeating eight hundred, at the same time attracting tigers and rejecting wolves, will commit more sins, and will have endless sequelae. This kind of change has the highest cost and the smallest profit.

In reform, we must start from the root and eliminate the cancer, and we must also give everyone the opportunity and motivation to repent, minimize the cost, and maximize the profit.

Therefore, every Chinese son and daughter should renounce and oppose the all-evil communism in spirit and action, and let the universal human values subtly expel evil, establish social justice and order, and realize common aspirations and well-being.

Therefore, every Chinese son and daughter should not regard a certain compatriot or a certain group as an enemy, and should not use fighting and violent means to solve problems. We should uphold Confucius' thought of "repaying grievances with directness", and use kindness and justice to solve problems. To solve problems, we should also adhere to Confucius' philosophy of "If you make a mistake and don't change it, that's the real mistake" .For the faults of others, don't pursue punishment, let's correct them together, and move forward together towards a better future!

CHAPTER 5: HUMANIZATION OF THE ARMY

1. Violence and war are a dying struggle when at the end of the road

People's feet walk the way, and people's hearts walk the reason. Road and truth make it easy for people to achieve their goals, and also make them safe and happy. Unreasonable existence not only hinders and hurts people, but also forces the energy to push people forward to be accumulated. This accumulation of energy is caused by obstacles and injuries, and it is also positively related to obstacles and injuries.

It is not the weight of one thousand catties that crushed the camel, but the last straw. What started the war was not deep hatred, but the humble fuse. Maybe you are a hero and invincible all your life, but in the end, you capsized in a small sewer and got ruined. Maybe you just stared at others, but you didn't know that he had had enough bullying on weekdays, and somehow he beat you up.

A mature society is a society that can resolve all contradictions with reason.

Road is the road that leads to the destination, the road and the rules of all existence, movement and change.

All beings have their own way, and the most closely related and most common for human are the way of heaven and the way of humanity.

The common point between the Road of Heaven and the Road of humanity is:meet the needs of others and other things, exchange your own needs, and live in harmony with each other.

In the human world, Road is everywhere. All human thoughts and actions are inseparable from Road, but everyone's Road is not the same.

In this society, everyone has their own understanding of "Road", everyone has a steel scale in their hearts, which is used to measure right and wrong, good and evil, and everyone has a principle in their hearts to guide their thoughts and action.

The truth that is recognized by everyone is the axiom, and the truth that completely conforms to the Road is the truth.

The driving force of the communication and interaction between people, groups of people and groups is their own needs, and the goal is the satisfaction of their own needs. When the principles of each other are incompatible and the Road is not connected, conflicts will arise.

A mature society will, under the premise of abiding by the Road, especially the Road of Heaven and humanity, and under the guidance of axioms, will maintain fairness and justice, judge right and wrong, good and evil, and coordinate demands and contradictions.

Therefore, a mature society can and should use reason to resolve all contradictions, rather than allowing contradictions and harm to accumulate on social members.

When people and people, people's groups and groups interact and interact with each other, contradictions and harms have arisen, and when people's society cannot resolve contradictions and uphold justice, there is no way to meet needs, resolve contradictions, and compensate for harm, and violence and war will arise.

So, Violence and war are a dying struggle when at the end of the road.

2. Violence and war are the road of no return without winners

(1) Self-proclaimed justice, fraternal love and dedication

Violence and war are the result of unmet needs, unresolved conflicts, and uncompensated injuries. Violence and war are a dying struggle when at the end of the road

Therefore, the initiators and participants of violence and war all think that they are right and should be, and they all have reasons. Even if he knows that this behavior is wrong, he will also take other people's faults , for a psychological comfort for himself.

War is a disaster for both sides. No matter what the cause is or who is the aggressor, it is the people of both sides who will ultimately suffer.

When the damage of war comes, people's fraternity and devotion will be stimulated, and the scope of disaster often determines the scope of fraternity and devotion.

In the face of the damage of the war, the fraternity and dedication of the two sides of the war are stimulated, and their collective consciousness is unprecedentedly strengthened. Therefore, once the war starts, it will become more and more intense, and eventually one side wins, while the other side will fail, or mutual destruction.

(2) The essence of sin cannot be concealed

Everything, and the movement and change of all existence, are generated from the needs of nature. Compared with existence, nature represents everything outside it. Therefore, as far as being is concerned, it is the right way to meet external needs in exchange for the satisfaction of own needs.

Therefore, violence and war that come from insatiable needs, irreparable harm, are contrary to the righteous way, and are contrary to the way of heaven, humanity, and justice.

As a result of violence, one or both parties are injured or even killed.

The result of the war is the suffering and death of a large number of the same kind, the huge consumption of social wealth, and the destruction of the natural ecological environment and all things.

If violence is evil, war is catastrophe.

Therefore, the initiators and participants of violence and war, even if they are full of reasons, cannot hide the essence of their evil deeds.

(3) The road of no return without a winner

Virtue, that is, obtaining the Road, is the reason and evidence for the existence and growth of all things. Virtue always follows the road. the Road generates all things, and it is based on needs. Virtue is that as an individual thing (person) obtains to make itself survive, the need for growth is to maintain and strengthen the needs of nature for oneself. The method is to fulfill the responsibilities and obligations that nature has given to oneself, and to do some good deeds that can be rewarded in the law of causality. Therefore, the meaning of virtue in traditional Chinese culture is basically It is equivalent to making contributions and doing good deeds. Virtue is not about obtaining things, nor is it plundering or occupying things and interests. If you can't get things right, you can't keep things, because that thing only belongs to the existence that produces and maintains it, need.

People's groups, like everything else, are determined by virtue for their existence and future prospects. Morality is an index to measure the degree of obtaining the road. The higher the degree of compliance with road, the more it can meet the needs of nature and everything in nature, and the deeper the morality will be.

Therefore, people and people's groups participated in violence and war, violated the Tao, and lost virtue. If you lose virtue, you will lose the basis for your existence and growth.

So, people and groups of people who are involved in violence and war do not have the desired outcome.

We have seen that many people suffered and even died in the war, and we have also seen that the victors and survivors of the war often suffered in the course of the war or in the years that followed. Different people and groups may suffer in different ways and time, but in the end the result is suffering.

People and groups of people who have participated in violence and war, no matter how much credit and glory they feel or be given by the group, can't change the fact that they have done evil. Heaven is vast, it seems to be very careless, but in the end it won't spare a bad man.

So, violence and war are the road of no return without winners.

3. Violence and war are the tools and reliance of evil

A wide range of injustice and unfair events in a society will intensify social contradictions. A normal society will fully respect the laws and trends of nature, fully respect the values from nature, and through mutual compromise within the society, to resolve conflicts.

In a dictatorial society, the source of injustice and injustice is the rulers. When social contradictions intensify, they do not think about social justice and fairness, the demands and well-being of the people, but their interests.

In order to safeguard their own interests, they will do whatever they can in the fields of culture, economy, and politics. When these means fail, they will resort to violence and war.

If the people are dissatisfied with the real hardship and injustice, then find a more formidable enemy for the people, divert the people's attention by intensifying external contradictions, or even initiate wars, and use nationalism and national interests to coerce the people, thereby weakening internal contradictions , to realize their continued oppression and enslavement of the people.

If the people are dissatisfied with the real hardship and injustice, they will pull out their guns. If the people are afraid, they will swallow their voices and continue to be oppressed and enslaved . Power comes from the barrel of a gun. This sentence fully reveals the nature of the dictator's superstition and reliance on force.

Of course, violence is the tool and reliance of evil, and it is also reflected in individual people, between small groups and small groups. Bring the other side to its knees by violence, Use violence to safeguard interests, and use violence to fight for your own fairness...

The essence of violence and war is evil. No matter what the reasons are for a person, a group, or a country, as long as violence or war is used, he (it) is evil.

A normal society has the responsibility to maintain the laws and trends of nature through cultural, economic and political means, to maintain the normal way of life of people, to maintain the values that come from nature and represent people's well-being, to maintain Social justice, fairness, and order, to prevent violence and war from occurring, to sanction the subjects who export violence and war, and to create a peaceful living environment for people.

4. Awakening from the war

(1) Heroes and Soldiers

Heroes are the object of worship and the dream of many people.

In fact, a hero is inseparable from the group to which he belongs. The heroes of a country are those who stand up for the interests of the country and even sacrifice themselves; the same is true for the heroes of a nation and an organization.

Enlarging the field of vision, we find that in human history, many people called heroes are actually executioners. For the benefit of his own country, nation, and organization, he slaughtered a large number of people from other countries, nations, and organizations. His fame was built on the bones of his kind. He is a hero in his own country, nation, and organization, but in other countries, nations, and organizations, he is a devil, a Satan-like existence.

In today's globalization of human social life, in today's frequent occurrence of natural disasters, and in today's extremely destructive weapons, what human beings need is no longer heroes who slaughter the same kind, but what human beings need is natural disasters A hero who stood up and even sacrificed himself in front of him;what human beings need is a true hero who stood up and even sacrificed himself to defend the peace of the human race.

A soldier is a person who defends his family and the country. Through war, he defends his compatriots, and defends the interests of his country, nation, and organization. They are all heroes. Soldiers are heroes, but heroes are not necessarily soldiers.

But soldiers, who belong to their own country, nation, and organization, and follow their own country, nation, and organization to conduct wars are killing the same kind. Therefore, soldiers can easily become the other side of heroes—the devil.

Therefore, if a soldier wants to be a pure hero, he should not fight and sacrifice for a certain country, nation, or organization, but should fight and sacrifice to maintain the peace of the human race and deal with natural disasters.

If it is said that every country, nation, and organization in the world has its own army and soldiers, it is the misfortune and stupidity of the entire human race; then, a soldier is willingly kidnapped by the consciousness of his own country, nation, and organization, and kills the same kind , is the ignorance and shame of this soldier.

(2) The sin and glory of ordinary citizens

Soldiers are supported by taxpayers, so a large part of the crimes and honors of soldiers belong to taxpayers.

This world is not peaceful, full of the threat of war and suffering, and it is inseparable from each of us, and each of us has a share of sin in it.

Therefore, each of us should not be kidnapped by the consciousness of our own country, nation, or organization, and we should not use our hard-earned money to support soldiers for our own country, nation, or organization, and let our own hands indirectly contaminate the same kind The blood brings sin to himself.

Soldiers are needed to maintain peace and order in this world, and soldiers are also needed to deal with disasters in this world. When soldiers stand up for world peace and order and to deal with world disasters, each of us has a share of glory in it.

Therefore , each of us must support the humanization of the army, support the soldiers for the sake of the human race, and oppose any country, nation, or organization having military power, so that every soldier can become a real hero of the human race. We are honored for feeding heroes.

(3) Awakening from the war

On both sides of the war, who does not think that he is just? Who has no reason to have to destroy the other?

As a result of the war, who did not lose? Who did not sacrifice? Isn't it all piles of corpses and drops of blood and sweat that fulfill the ambitions of very few people?

There are many people who instigate war, but how many are willing to let him carry a gun and die on the battlefield? Is it not their evil and selfishness to instigate war?

My own country has become stronger and has defeated the enemy country. Most people, apart from bragging capital, what else have they added? After defeating the enemy and slaughtering the same clan, isn't his world still devastated?

Dear people, wake up! Please don't let ideology, national feelings and organizational concepts kidnap you. Please don't be pathetic and take it for granted to do evil. Please cherish your life, your dependent peers and your home!

5. Humanization of the Army

(1) The long-term existence and prosperity of human society requires the humanization of the army

Human society needs values, such as freedom, democracy, equality, justice, diversity, and moderate competition, as well as cultural, economic and political systems to maintain the normal order and vitality of human society, so that human society can exist and thrive for a long time.

This determines that there must be a large number of cultural, economic and political contradictions in human society.

War, as the parties involved in various contradictions, a desperate struggle, as an evil path that violates the way of heaven and humanity, is easily launched by people and groups of people due to their own selfishness, greed, and evil.

Once a war is launched, the only way for the relevant parties is to use violence to control violence and to end war with war, and human society will lose the normal way to resolve conflicts with reason.

War is bound to have catastrophic consequences.

Therefore, human society needs the humanization of the army to maintain the normal order and vitality of human society, so that human society can exist and prosper for a long time.

(2) All countries retain their armies, and war is inevitable

Any country in the world with a strong military is a threat to other countries and will make other countries sleepless.

Every country in the world has a powerful army, which is a threat to all countries and will make all countries sleepless.

Under the leadership of the sense of opposition, the security of one's own country and organization is often built on the basis of the sleeplessness of other countries and organizations.

NATO has expanded to Russia's doorstep, Russia's dorm room is uneasy, and a nuclear power is still like this. Ukraine is at the border with a nuclear power. If it is not unsafe, why would you want to join NATO for asylum? Russia is sleepless, but as a nuclear power with the second largest military force in the world, who would easily start a war with it? How much of the invasion of Ukraine was really in the interest of the Russian people and the country? Didn't the anti-war demonstrations of the Russian people fully illustrate this?

As a product of the US-Soviet hegemony, should NATO withdraw from the stage of history after the disintegration of the Soviet Union? If NATO withdraws from the stage of history and faces a powerful Russia, will European countries also have trouble sleeping?

Therefore, as long as every country in the world retains its military, and there are military alliances established by individual countries, military competition in this world is inevitable, and it is inevitable that it will eventually escalate into war.

If the United Nations cannot control the military, it cannot control the military battles between countries. This is like a person who is ill and has a tumor, but cannot take the initiative to heal, and can only wait for death with his eyes open.

This is the tragedy of the entire human society.

(3) The world cannot be without an army

Violence and war are the dying struggle of human beings at the end of the road, and the highest manifestation of human social contradictions.

The army is a tool of war, but it is also the biggest support for maintaining the normal social order of mankind.

If the whole world cancels the army, then the police of various countries will assume the role of the army, and the world will always be immersed in the threat of war. If the police are abolished all over the world, then violence and small-scale conflicts will be unchecked, will spread like a tumor, and the world will become hell.

Therefore, the world cannot be without an army.

In fact, in human history, the ownership of the army has been continuously expanded with the progress of civilization.

From primitive tribes to whole tribes, from feudal states to whole countries, from different political parties to nationalization of the army, the ownership of the army has been expanding, because only by expanding the ownership of the army can internal wars be avoided.

So, in today's world, the best way to eliminate the threat of war is to humanize the military.

(4) Humanity cannot afford a nuclear war

With the development of human civilization, the lethality of weapons is constantly improving, especially the existence of nuclear weapons, which has reached the point where it can destroy human beings.

It is an indisputable fact that mankind cannot afford a large-scale nuclear war.

Similar to the reasons for the humanization of the military, nuclear weapons also need to be humanized, and the world's need for the humanization of nuclear weapons is more urgent than the humanization of the military.

(5) Humanization of the army must begin in the free world

The human foot follows the Road, and the human heart follows the principle.

Road and principle is the way of life. Therefore, in each of our lives, the road and the principle has a very deep precipitation, so each of us naturally knows where justice lies, what is right and wrong, and what is good and evil.

Equality, freedom, and democracy are values that come from nature, and nature also has a deep precipitation in everyone's vitality.

If there is no brainwashing propaganda and education, no temptation of unreasonable interests, and no threat of violence, everyone will choose equality, freedom and democracy.

Therefore, brainwashing, transfer of interests, and violent suppression are the three knives of dictators. The army is the most important and ultimate support for the dictator, because without the violent suppression of the army, the first two knives would have no vitality .

Therefore, a dictator will never give up the army voluntarily, and in a dictatorial country, people have no ability to make the dictator give up the army.

In a free country, people have more equality, freedom, and democracy, have more correct cognition of the truth of the world, and have more sense of justice. As long as people can fully realize the danger of the state mastering the army and the urgency of the humanization of the army, it is relatively feasible to first form the integration of the army among free countries.

Therefore, the humanization of the army should be carried out in two steps. The first is the integration of the army in the free world.

6. Strictly prevent world dictatorship

(1) Everyone is responsible

The increasingly serious natural disasters faced by mankind and the rising probability of mankind being destroyed by war call for the awakening of human consciousness, for the expansion of the power of the United Nations, and for the humanization of the military, especially nuclear weapons, to bridge differences and safeguard Justice, limit the struggle, so as to deal with the current crisis and achieve the long-term existence and prosperity of the human race.

And this is essentially a centralized process.

With the continuous improvement of the level of human science and technology, especially the increase in the lethality of weapons, people will increasingly lose the ability to resist dictatorship, especially military dictatorship.

The more scientific and technological means the dictator has, the more he can strengthen his control over the people, the more he can eliminate dissidents when them is weak, the greater the crimes he can commit, and the greater the suffering of the people.

The military dictatorship is even more serious. Even in the age of cold weapons, to overthrow a tyranny and restore heaven and humanity requires a shockingly large number of similar lives. Today, when weapons are extremely lethal, the people simply do not have the ability to fight against the army controlled by the dictator.

Therefore, with the development of human society, it is more and more important to maintain the values and cultural, economic and political systems of equality, freedom and democracy, and moderate competition.

Therefore, for dictatorships, especially military dictatorships, a situation must be formed in which everyone shouts and resists. Otherwise, once they succeed, not only will everyone not be able to escape the fate of being oppressed and enslaved, but the entire human society will be doomed.

(2) Responsibilities of Soldiers

Every soldier is the son and daughter of the people and is supported by the people with blood and sweat. Therefore, every soldier should be loyal to the people and safeguard the interests and safety of the people.

This is the way of heaven and humanity, and it is also the innate duty of a soldier.

It is the natural duty of the soldiers to safeguard the interests and life safety of the people and fight against any form of threat to the interests and safety of the people! Safeguarding the interests and life safety of the people, and shedding blood for the interests and safety of the people is the honor of the soldiers!

At present, some troops, loyal to a certain country or organization, obey the orders of their superiors, and brutally suppress the unarmed people at every turn. This is the violation of heaven and humanity by the army and soldiers, a serious dereliction of duty and a loss of humanity and conscience!

It is right for soldiers to obey the orders of their superiors. Otherwise, the army will lose its order, soldiers with weapons will become a disaster for society, and the army and soldiers will lose the value and rationality of their existence.

However, if the superior's orders deviate from heaven, humanity and his natural mission, his superior has become a dictator or an accomplice of a dictator. Executing orders becomes a crime; Refusing orders is the maintenance of heaven, humanity and one's natural duty; Eliminating dictators and their minions is the recovery of heaven and humanity, the fulfillment of military sacred mission and military supreme glory!

(3) Anti-dictatorship mechanism

Dictatorship is a rape of heaven and humanity, a trampling on the normal human order, and a crime against the people!

Therefore, it is the innate responsibility of a mature society to establish and maintain an anti-dictatorship mechanism.

The realization of any goal of human beings must follow the paths and rules of nature, and science is an effective means of cognition for human beings to the paths and rules of nature.

Therefore, to establish and maintain an anti-dictatorship mechanism, science must be respected, and scientists must be reasonably involved.

Violence and war, in their essence, are evil, and their results are disasters.

Therefore, to establish and maintain an anti-dictatorship mechanism, we cannot use violence to suppress violence and war to stop war, but should be done on the premise of non-violence.

The army will always be the dictator's biggest and ultimate support.

Therefore, establishing and maintaining an anti-dictatorship mechanism, establishing an anti-military dictatorship mechanism, cutting off the relationship between the dictator and the army, and eliminating the conditions for dictatorship in the army should be the top priority.

The fundamental purpose of establishing and maintaining the anti-dictatorship mechanism is to maintain the way of heaven and humanity, to maintain the normal social order of mankind, to maintain the long-term existence and prosperity of the human race, and to safeguard the interests and life safety of the vast number of human compatriots.

Therefore, to establish and maintain an anti-dictatorship mechanism, we should tolerate the past and face the future. Leave the existing dictators with tolerance and opportunities to repent and repent, eliminate the conditions for the emergence, existence and development of dictatorships, and block the path for the emergence, existence and development of dictatorships.

Establishing and maintaining an anti-dictatorship mechanism is an eternal and important issue facing the human race, and no theory can be perfect.

Therefore, human society and everyone has the responsibility and obligation to participate, and with the strength of the entire human race, formulate and continuously adjust the anti-dictatorship mechanism to realize the long-term existence and prosperity of the human race.

ABOUT THE AUTHOR

I was born in a Christian family and grew up in the Gospel of God. In college, under the guidance of teachers, I systematically studied Eastern philosophy. This book is a combination of eastern and western thoughts. Let love fill the world, is my lifelong ideal.

www.ingramcontent.com/pod-product-compliance
Lightning Source LLC
Chambersburg PA
CBHW051445150726
48000CB00005B/2251